A complete guide to the techniques, gear, history and philosophy of tenkara, the Japanese method of fly-fishing. **A manifesto on fly-fishing simplicity.**

tenkara

—
the
book
—

Daniel Galhardo

DESIGN & ILLUSTRATIONS BY

JEREMY SHELLHORN

Published by
Tenkara Press, an imprint of Tenkara, L.L.C.
www.tenkarausa.com/publishing

Design and illustrations by Jeremy Shellhorn
Edited by Bevin Wallace
Photos by Daniel W. Galhardo, unless otherwise noted

Library of Congress Cataloging-in-Publication Data on file
2017901905

ISBN 978-0-9987092-0-8 (print)
ISBN 978-0-9987092-1-5 (digital)

Printed in the United States of America
To buy this book in bulk quantities, email info@tenkarausa.com or call 888.i.tenkara

table of contents

The author has some fun after fishing with Mr. Yuzo Sebata in Japan.

how to read this book

This book begins with a quick guide that will show you the basic things you need to know to get started fishing with a tenkara rod.

Then throughout the book I expand on the basics of equipment and technique, and share just about everything I've learned from teachers in Japan and from teaching thousands of people how to tenkara.

It may seem contradictory that a simpler method of fly-fishing would require this many pages to explain. And it doesn't. You can grasp most of what you need from the first few pages and first paragraphs of each section. But, I do go into the very nuanced details of the method for those who are interested.

Throughout the book I share my experiences learning tenkara through recounting stories. That is my attempt to take you on my personal journey of learning the method with its masters in Japan. It is my hope that the stories, the philosophy, the history and culture of tenkara will be remembered more than the instructions themselves.

A lot of the information in this book is there to activate what will likely come to you instinctively. When you go fishing with your tenkara rod I hope you will not have to consciously think about what you learned in this book and that you will experience fishing without having to think too much about it. That is the best way to experience tenkara.

This book is interactive and takes advantage of all the resources we have created over the years and the ones we will create in the future. The main thing you will notice in the book is the inclusion of QR (quick response) codes.

These QR codes will take you to resources on the web, typically videos, to help illustrate the topic discussed more clearly than my words can.

How to use the QR codes

All you need to do is go to your app browser and search for "QR reader". There will be many free options available. Download one. Test it by opening the app and scanning the code on this page. It will take you to the book's main resource page on our website.

Scan this QR code to watch a video.

Scanning the different codes throughout the book (or, alternatively, typing the URL provided) will take you to the complementary resource*. For example, on page 143 I discuss casting. I can talk all I want about casting yet still leave you wondering what the cast looks like. Scanning the code with your phone or tablet and watching a short video will help make things much clearer. If the QR code ever stops working, or you don't have a mobile or tablet handy, simply type the URL provided below the code.

Book updates

If I make any changes or updates to this book, these changes will be posted on www.tenkarausa.com/book. Check in periodically, and follow Tenkara USA on social media and our blog for updates.

How to Set Up Your Tenkara Rod

Scan QR code to access a short video on setting up your rod.

10kara.co/1

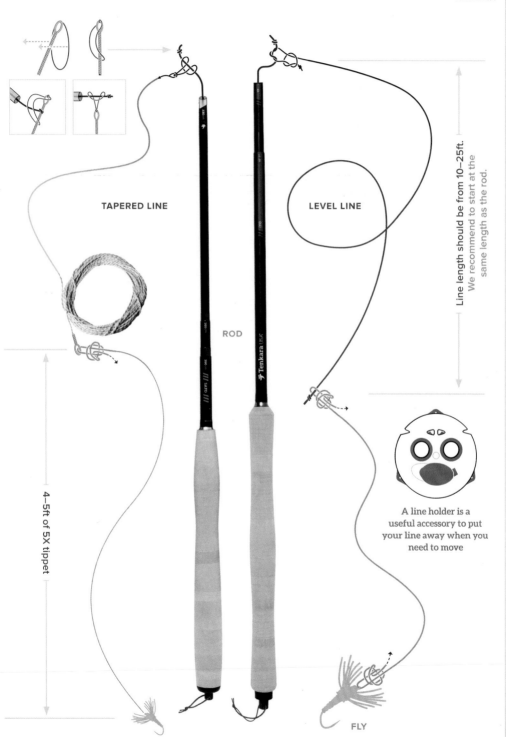

TAPERED LINE

LEVEL LINE

ROD

Line length should be from 10–25ft. We recommend to start at the same length as the rod.

4–5ft of 5X tippet

A line holder is a useful accessory to put your line away when you need to move

FLY

Anytime you learn a new knot, I highly recommend sitting at home and tying the knot several times in order to understand it and get the physical memory for the knot so that you don't struggle when out in the water.

Scan this QR code
to watch a video on how
to tie the one knot.

10kara.com/2

How to tie the "One Knot" in 4 steps

1 Form a loop with the tag to the right.

2 Make two wraps around main line. If you are securing the knot to a loop or fly, pass the line through before tying the knot.

3 Feed the working end through the two loops.

4 Pull the knot tight by holding both ends and pulling the loop.

How to Read Water and Find Fish

TENKARA QUICK GUIDE | Scan QR code to access a short video on reading water.

10kara.co/3

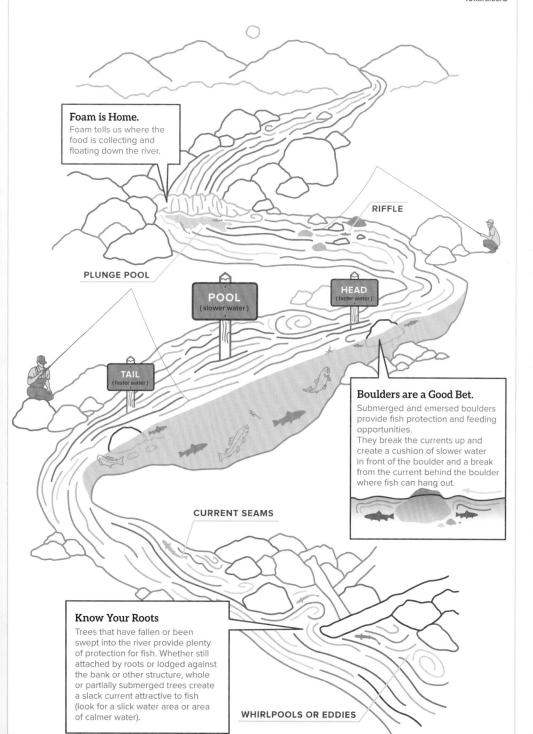

Foam is Home.
Foam tells us where the food is collecting and floating down the river.

RIFFLE

PLUNGE POOL

POOL (slower water)

HEAD (faster water)

TAIL (faster water)

Boulders are a Good Bet.
Submerged and emersed boulders provide fish protection and feeding opportunities.
They break the currents up and create a cushion of slower water in front of the boulder and a break from the current behind the boulder where fish can hang out.

CURRENT SEAMS

Know Your Roots
Trees that have fallen or been swept into the river provide plenty of protection for fish. Whether still attached by roots or lodged against the bank or other structure, whole or partially submerged trees create a slack current attractive to fish (look for a slick water area or area of calmer water).

WHIRLPOOLS OR EDDIES

In simplified terms, reading water can be boiled down to understanding that currents bring food to fish and that fish don't want to spend too much energy fighting those currents. The best places to cast a fly will often be where there is a meeting of these two conditions. Casting into calm water (which allows fish to stay in an area without spending too much energy) near faster water (which is bringing food down to the fish) is usually a good approach.

In tumbling mountain streams, target the calmest waters you see since fish do not want to fight very heavy currents. Features such as boulders and logs form an easy place for fish to stay put and protected while still having access to food. Also, target features that can allow a fish to stay in one area, such as behind rocks (including larger submerged rocks), in front of rocks, and in waters along the banks. Learn to identify other smaller features such as foam ("foam is home" as they say), whirlpools, and subtle water slicks that are just a tad slower than the faster waters around them.

While fishing, consider casting first toward the features at the tail of the pool (downstream end), and working your way up. Don't ignore very small pockets of water; those are the ones most anglers ignore because they are hard to fish with rod and reel, but they are easy to fish with tenkara.

In slower-moving water with fewer features, fish may be in a wider area. Target deeper areas, where the water may slow down a bit, as well as areas that offer protection to fish, such as undercut banks.

About Tenkara Flies

10kara.co/4

Any fly can be used with tenkara. In fact, most tenkara anglers in Japan stick with only one fly pattern. Daniel Galhardo, founder of Tenkara USA, fishes with only these four tenkara flies. The beauty in tenkara flies lies in their simplicity and versatility.

Amano Kebari

Ishigaki Kebari

Oki Kebari

Takayama Kebari

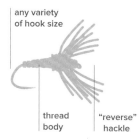

any variety
of hook size

thread
body

"reverse"
hackle

A *"Sakasa Kebari"* **fly is easy to tie and very effective.**

SUGGESTIVE V. IMITATIVE

Tenkara flies don't imitate anything in particular, yet they suggest just about any bug in the water. This suggestive rather than imitative approach leads to incredible versatility, which in turn allows for simplicity.

Benefits of reverse hackle flies or "sakasa" kebari:

• incredibly easy and quick to tie
• looks buggy under water as hackle stays open
• the ability to impart motion by pulsating the fly and closing and opening the hackle

How to tie a *Sakasa Kebari* in 6 steps

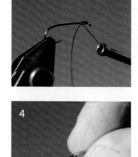

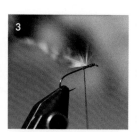

1. Wrap thread 3-5 turns to make a head on the hook. Cut excess thread

2. Secure the hackle with 2-3 wraps of thread and cut off feather stem.

3. Wrap hackle 3-4 times toward back.

4. Secure hackle with 4 wraps of thread. Push hackle forward.

5. Wrap back toward the end of the hook to build the body of the fly.

6. Tie the thread off with a half hitch or whip finish.

Yoshikazu Fujioka ties a "*sakasa kebari*" at the 2015 Tenkara Summit.

How to Cast and Land a Fish

Scan QR code to access a short video on casting,

10kara.co/5

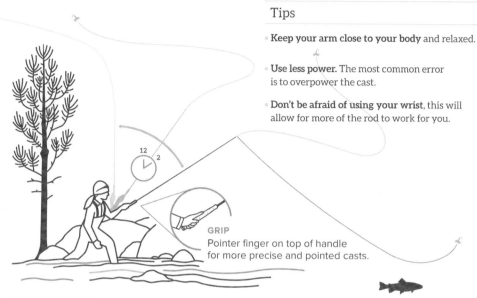

Tips

- **Keep your arm close to your body** and relaxed.

- **Use less power.** The most common error is to overpower the cast.

- **Don't be afraid of using your wrist**, this will allow for more of the rod to work for you.

GRIP
Pointer finger on top of handle for more precise and pointed casts.

OVERHAND CAST

Casting is very intuitive. Throw the line back by moving the rod to a vertical position (12 o'clock). Very briefly stop the rod to let the line load the rod and immediately move the rod down in front of you to the 2 o"clock position. This will throw the line forward and take the fly with it.

10kara.com/6

LANDING A FISH

Angle the rod back to bring the fish toward you. If the line is longer than the rod, grab the line and bring the fish as close to you as you can. When the fish is close to you, wet your hand and cradle it or net it.

Tim Gasperak brings in a wild Colorado brownie in Eldorado Canyon.

How to Handle a Fish and Remove a Hook

Scan QR code to access a short video on releasing.

10kara.co/7

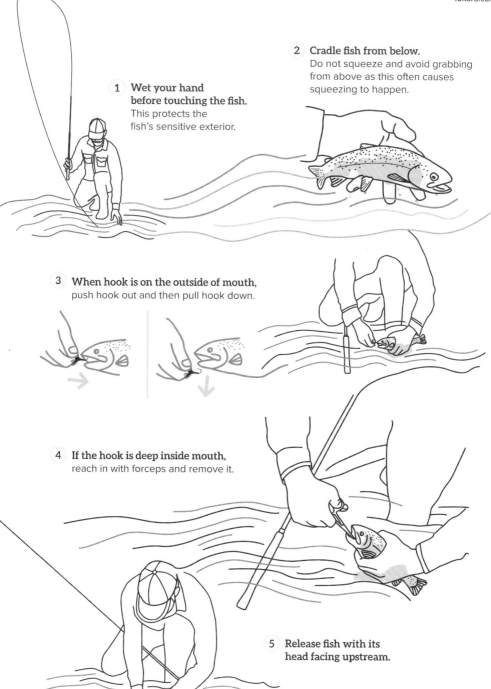

1 **Wet your hand before touching the fish.**
This protects the fish's sensitive exterior.

2 **Cradle fish from below.**
Do not squeeze and avoid grabbing from above as this often causes squeezing to happen.

3 **When hook is on the outside of mouth,**
push hook out and then pull hook down.

4 **If the hook is deep inside mouth,**
reach in with forceps and remove it.

5 **Release fish with its head facing upstream.**

Brian Flemming

introduction
—

In 2008 I visited Japan for the first time. I had recently married Margaret, a second-generation Japanese American from Los Angeles, and we were planning a trip to visit her grandparents who live in Yamagata, a city nestled in the mountains north of Tokyo. At this point I had been fly-fishing for about 10 years, and one thing I knew I wanted to do on that trip was to fly-fish.

Inspecting a map of Japan, I looked at the mountains and streams with an eager angler's eye.

Japan is not only surrounded by water, but its mountains contain a huge amount of streams and rivers. With so much water, I assumed that there must be a rich fly-fishing tradition in Japan.

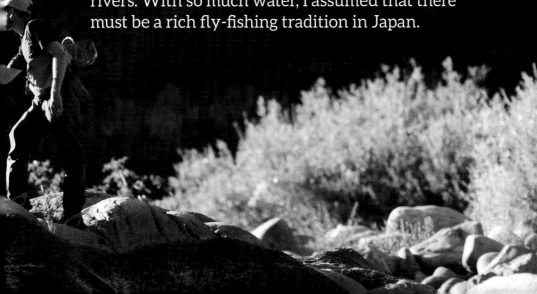

With that assumption I started researching fly-fishing in Japan. I soon came across a book called *Angling in Japan*, which described the huge variety of fishing methods found in Japan. Among its pages was a photograph of an angler fishing a mountain stream. Below there was a photograph of a native Japanese trout, the *yamame*. The book also discussed anglers not using reels, but using flies to catch trout. I didn't realize it then, but I was looking at tenkara.

With more research I discovered this was a method of fishing that was still alive in Japan. When we visited Margaret's grandparents in Yamagata I made sure to stop at a tackle shop to see tenkara in person. While I knew what tenkara was supposed to look like, seeing the equipment in person and learning from the store's clerk about tenkara made everything click.

The store was pretty large and had equipment for all types of fishing. On the lower portion of a shelf there were six or seven tenkara rods. The clerk pulled one out of its packaging and showed me the telescopic rod. It was long when fully extended, but I immediately thought about how perfect it would be for backpacking when he telescoped it back to its 20-inch collapsed size. He then explained the only other things I needed were a spool of line, some tippet, and flies; so he took me to the section in the store where the line was, and then the fly section. When he showed me how to set up a rod I noticed how quick rigging it all together was (it usually takes me about 45 seconds to set up the rod and start fishing). And, when he showed me how to cast with a tenkara rod, I realized I was looking at fly-fishing, just much simpler.

I bought a tenkara rod from him, brought it back to the U.S., and started tenkara fishing. I started teaching myself how to use the equipment, which was pretty intuitive. Looking back, on my first couple of outings I just used the tenkara rod setup the same way I used my rod and reel by laying line on the water and mending. Then I realized the long rod allowed me to fish it a bit differently; I could keep the rod tip up and achieve very good drifts without currents dragging my line. Soon I was catching a lot more fish than I did before.

After years of mending lines and unwrapping them from around my leg, I realized what my fishing had been missing: simplicity. With tenkara fly-fishing was simple, unencumbered. Tenkara brought back childhood memories of fishing for fun. And I was fascinated by the thought that this simpler form of fly-fishing was also more effective than the fly-fishing I knew.

It occurred to me that I couldn't be the only fly-fisherman craving simplicity. So, in late 2008 I started creating Tenkara USA and on April 12, 2009 I opened for business and started telling the tenkara story and selling the few items truly needed for fly-fishing.

From the beginning, I knew Tenkara USA would be more than just an equipment manufacturer. We would focus on sharing the rich story of tenkara, the techniques, and on the message that fly-fishing can be very simple.

Since starting Tenkara USA, my passion for tenkara has only grown. I am determined to introduce the complete method of tenkara, honor its history, and make sure we do not throw away hundreds of years of refined techniques. But I also understand that people will want to experiment with their own techniques, which may deviate from how tenkara has been traditionally practiced in Japan. With this book, and with Tenkara USA, my mission is to provide a starting place for people in search of a simpler way to fish so they can find their own tenkara.

It is not an exaggeration to say that tenkara has created a movement within the sport of fly-fishing. Tenkara has inspired many people to take up fly-fishing, an activity that is often perceived as complicated, intimidating, and inaccessible. It has also allowed experienced fly anglers all over the world to make fly-fishing a simpler experience and to learn how to rely more on their technique and knowledge than on equipment.

Since that first trip in 2008, I have gone to Japan yearly to learn more about tenkara, and I have hosted tenkara anglers from Japan here on home waters. With these interactions I am constantly reminded how much there is to learn. Below the simple surface of tenkara, there is a multitude of layers comprised of nuanced techniques, history and culture. This is the contradiction of simplicity: As we seek to limit and simplify the equipment we use, we are put in a position to better learn to use what we have.

The techniques and stories I share in this book are a result of learning from several teachers in Japan and from my own experiences teaching tenkara to others. I have strived to find a balance between sharing everything I know about tenkara while still conveying its simplicity and making it accessible to you. My hope is that through this book you will discover tenkara and come out on the other side with a simpler kit, more focus on your experience, and more fish at the end of your line.

Daniel and Dr. Ishigaki
fish together in Colorado.

Brad Clement

A Story From My Childhood

Fishing was an integral part of my childhood. We lived about an hour from the ocean and had easy access to ponds, streams, and lakes near home. Fishing was always the preferred way to spend a free weekend.

In fact, one of my earliest memories is of fishing with a plastic fishing rod toy. The rod was about two or three feet long; it had a simple plastic reel built into it and thick cord wrapped around it. At the end of the line there was a large plastic fish. I remember standing next to my father while he fished a small creek, lowering my red plastic fish into the water and proudly raising it—my imagination making the fish come to life.

My hometown of Curitiba in Southern Brazil has a large Japanese community. Japanese immigrants had come to Brazil in the early 1900s in search of work and land to farm. I had several Japanese-Brazilian friends growing up, and I knew they and their families liked fishing. When we saw them fishing, it seemed like they usually out-fished us.

When I was nine or 10 years old we went to the park for an afternoon of fishing. Across the lake from us were two men of Japanese descent. They sat on chairs in the sun and were catching a lot of fish. Although I remember we were doing okay ourselves, at one point my dad turned to me with a mix of frustration and admiration and said, "*Se quiser mesmo aprender a pescar, tem que pedir pra um Japones te ensinar.*" ("If you really wanna learn how to fish, you need to ask a Japanese person to teach you.")

I remembered this day like it was yesterday now, but I didn't think about it until a couple of years after I started learning from Dr. Ishigaki and other Japanese anglers. It's amazing how things have turned out. Perhaps subconsciously I took my father's advice to heart.

My Teachers

Beyond the idea of using just a rod, line and fly, there is little chance I would be able to truly understand how efficient tenkara can be and to share the techniques used in tenkara if it were not by learning the method directly from the masters in Japan.

I'm not interested in reinventing a method of fishing, but rather I'd prefer to share the centuries of refinements in techniques along with its history and culture. While tenkara is simple to pick up, there are nuances in the technique that have been passed down through generations or learned by individual anglers through their decades of experience. It would be a shame to not learn from them.

In a play of words tenkara is said to have "ten colors." Each tenkara angler will fish a bit differently from each other, showing slight variations in tackle and technique. Learning from several tenkara anglers in Japan has allowed me to pick up on these small differences. It has also allowed me to understand what gives tenkara its essence and what is truly the meaning of tenkara.

Over the years, the people whom I consider to be some of the masters of tenkara have welcomed me into their lives and have taught me most of what I know. In the following pages are the people from whom I have learned tenkara.

Dr. Hisao Ishigaki

It can only be seen as fate that soon after I discovered tenkara, I met Dr. Hisao Ishigaki , the most prominent tenkara angler in Japan. Dr. Ishigaki had been invited to speak about tenkara in the Catskills Fly Fishing Center and Museum in New York. As soon as I heard the master of tenkara from Japan was coming I booked a ticket and went there to meet him. We met on May 22nd, 2009, exactly 40 days after I launched Tenkara USA.

Dr. Ishigaki is tall and has a strong build, but his warmth ensures there is never a vestige of an intimidating person in him. He laughs easily and his sense of humor crosses over any language barriers in a way that puts anyone near him at ease. Any anxiety I had before meeting such an important person dissipated the moment we shook hands. As we sat together at the museum and chatted about my dreams in introducing tenkara outside of Japan. He said he would become my *tenkara otto-san*, or "tenkara father".

Indeed, Dr. Ishigaki has become my "tenkara father". I enjoyed his presentation and demo the next day, and then we spent the day after that fishing together. It was immediately apparent he wanted to teach me what he knew. Since then we have fished together every year, at least once a year when I visit Japan, and on multiple occasions when he's visited the U.S.. Most of the things I will share in this book are derived from the teachings of Dr. Ishigaki.

Dr. Ishigaki is the full embodiment of tenkara. He started learning tenkara in the late 1970s, and is one of the few people alive today who learned tenkara directly from the previous generation of tenkara "masters." Dr. Ishigaki absorbed and incorporated the style, techniques, and spirit of these anglers.

Dr. Ishigaki enjoying the fishing in South Boulder Creek, Colorado.

Mr. Katsutoshi Amano started fishing with tenkara as a young teenager; in his 60s, he maintained a youthful laughter and a child-like approach to fishing. He taught me the importance of rhythm in pulsating my *sakasa kebari*. Learning that another of Japan's most recognized tenkara anglers uses only one type of fly—of the exact same size, color, and shape—and that he ties each one with no vise has given me confidence to further simplify my tenkara.

Mr. Masami Sakakibara is also known as the *tenkara no oni*, or "tenkara demon". He earned the nickname due to the very serious and focused expression he keeps when he's fishing. Sakakibara-san helped me understand and get a bit closer to mastering the tenkara cast. Sakakibara-san's effortless and precise casts were a revelation to me, showing me how easy casting a tenkara line can be when you let your brain do most of the work. I have since shared his technique with numerous students.

Mr. Yoshikazu Fujioka often wears a fishing vest adorned with the patch for his fly-fishing club, the Tsuttenkai. The club's tagline of "Jolly Fishers" fits Fujioka-san very well. He shared with me his passion and great knowledge of tenkara flies. His website, http://www.hi-ho.ne.jp/amago/, was one of the only resources I could count on when I first started learning about tenkara. His jovial spirit and interest in the history of tenkara have made him great company whenever I visit Japan.

Mr. Yuzo Sebata always wears the traditional Japanese *kasa* hat with a stash of flies hidden in his hat. His rock-hopping skills belie his age (73 as I write this). Mr. Sebata developed legendary status in Japan for the steep cliffs and remote streams he fishes and the "Sebata magic"—a term thrown around in fishing circles in Japan due to Sabata's ability to coax fish out of unlikely places. His adventures have continued to inspire me to enjoy tenkara for fishing's sake and to "go deeper upstream" in search of fish.

Mr. Yoshimaru Shotaro was 89-years old when I first met him in 2011 during a two-month stay in the village of Maze. He shared his experience of learning tenkara by "stealing" a professional angler's technique from a distance over a summer when he was about 12 years old. When I met him he hadn't fished in about three years due to failing legs. As we talked about tenkara, I could see he missed the water. A spark came to his eyes and he invited me to fish with him. Watching him cast a line and his flies into the water gave me a glimpse into the history of tenkara. Mr. Shotaro passed away in late 2016. I cherish my memory of meeting him.

part
one

about tenkara

What is Tenkara?

Tenkara is the Japanese method of fly-fishing that uses only a rod, line, and fly and no reel. It is a fixed-line method of fishing, meaning the line is of fixed length and is tied to the tip of the rod. Tenkara originated in the hands of commercial anglers of Japan as an effective way to catch trout in mountain streams.

Tenkara shows us that simplicity and effectiveness are not mutually exclusive. In this section, I offer an overview of the tools and method, its history and philosophy so that you will understand tenkara. Throughout the book I'll delve deeper into each aspect of the subject.

The word "*tenkara*"

In Japanese, tenkara is written: テンカラ (te n ka ra). It is pronounced: ten (as in the number), ka (like the first part of the word "car"), and ra (a very soft ra, very close to da). Someone familiar with Japanese may read the word in Romanized characters "*ten kara*" or hear it out of context and take it to mean "from heaven," where *ten* is "heaven", and *kara* means "from." However, use of the katakana system of writing makes it unclear what the intended meaning was supposed to be.

There are several theories for how the name tenkara came about. According to Mr. Yoshikazu Fujioka, "Some say it's because tenkara means 'from the sky,' suggestive of the way the flies [fall] into the water from above. Others say it came from the word 'tengara,' which is an entirely different method of fishing for Ayu (sweet fish) introduced to Japan from China.

SAY TENKARA

10kara.co/7A

Still others say it's derived from a game [called] ken-ken, in which children hop around on one leg inside a circle drawn on the ground and tenkara fishermen hop from rock to rock in the streams. It's pronounced differently in various regional dialects, including Chingara, Shinkara and Tsunkara. I prefer this theory, because the playfulness appeals to me."

テンカラ

The story I've heard the most often is how one day a professional tenkara fisherman was casting his fly around a stream and catching a lot of fish. Someone not familiar with the method approached him and asked, "How do you catch so many fish?" The tenkara angler replied, "Well, at the end of my line I have this fly I tied using a feather and thread. I cast it, the fish sees the fly coming from heaven (ten kara), and when it lands, it bites." And so the word spread in that region.

Tenkara was not always "tenkara" everywhere in Japan. Before it became widely called tenkara throughout Japan, this method of mountain stream fishing with a fly was most commonly known as *kebari tsuri*. *Tsuri* is the Japanese word for fishing and kebari literally means "feathered/haired hook" and is the word for an artificial fly. As western fly-fishing got introduced in Japan after WWII and tenkara saw a surge of popularity as a sport in the 1970s, there came a need to differentiate the two methods of fishing with a fly. At that time more magazine articles and books started being written about fishing, and *tenkara* became the word of choice for the native method of fly-fishing.

NOTE: It should also be noted that the term *tenkara* refers the method of fishing (and since it is not a proper noun I keep it in lower case, including in the title of the book). The brand I created to introduce tenkara outside of Japan is Tenkara USA. There has been a lot of confusion with a large number of new companies in the market using the term "tenkara" in their names. Tenkara USA is the original tenkara rod company in the US.

Tenkara Gear

The equipment used in tenkara is designed specifically for the method. The rods, lines, and flies used in tenkara fishing have been tweaked and improved over time with very specific functions in mind.

Tenkara Rods

Tenkara rods range from about 9 feet to over 14 feet in length when fully extended, with 12 feet being the average length. The rods are telescopic, so a 12-foot rod may fit inside a 20-inch segment.

Even though the length of a tenkara rod is intimidating at first, particularly for those with a background in western fly-fishing, I recommend using the longest rod you can. I hardly ever use a rod shorter than 13 feet where I live in Colorado. Short rods have their place, too. I consider any tenkara rod under 10 feet long to be short. When you find yourself scrambling up to a small tributary covered in trees, a shorter rod, such as the Tenkara USA Rhodo, can be handy.

Keep in mind that with a longer rod you always have the option to hold the rod above the handle. Choking up on the grip in this manner can easily get your rod to perform at about 2 feet shorter. This way your 12-foot long rod fishes at 10 feet long when you so desire but will still have good reach for when the water opens up.

There are also adjustable tenkara rods, which are designed to be fished at different lengths. These rods offer a great amount of versatility—they are long rods when the stream is open, shorter when the water gets tighter. The Tenkara USA Sato and Rhodo rods are probably the most popular tenkara rods around for this reason.

You will learn more about tenkara rods on page 63

Tenkara Lines

At the tip of a tenkara rod, there is a piece of soft braided material called the lillian. The tenkara line is tied to this material.

Tenkara lines are designed specifically for tenkara with three main goals in mind: tenkara lines must be heavy enough to cast, but as light as possible to allow more line to be kept off the water. Lastly, they must also be very visible.

There are different types of tenkara lines; the two most commonly used are tenkara tapered lines and tenkara level lines. Tapered lines are easier to cast but must be made or bought at specific lengths. Level lines, on the other hand, come in a spool and can be cut to the desired length. The type of line chosen is primarily based on personal preference, with some people enjoying the soft and easy cast provided by a tapered line while others enjoy the versatility of level lines and the fact that by being light they stay off the water more easily.

The length of the tenkara line is fixed while fishing (though it is very easy to switch a shorter line for a longer one when necessary). The length used is determined by the angler and sometimes dictated by the water one is fishing. There are no exact formulas here, but typically I recommend starting with a line length similar to the length of the rod plus 4 feet of tippet. With more experience, and when a larger or more open body of water calls for it, gradually experiment with longer lines.

At the end of the tenkara line, whichever type and length of line, the angler will tie approximately 4 feet of tippet (3 to 5 feet of tippet is acceptable). No leader is necessary; tippet serves as a transition between the main tenkara line and the fly. While multiple weights of tippet exist and can be used with tenkara, I keep it simple and stick with tippet rated to approximately 5 lbs. of strength (5X tippet) and use nylon tippet.

You will learn more about tenkara lines on page 78

Tenkara Flies

Onto the end of the tippet, one ties a fly, which is an artificial representation of bugs tied on a hook with thread and feathers.

Any normal trout fly can be used in tenkara. If you already fly-fish you will be pleased to know your favorite dry flies, nymphs, terrestrial flies, and even streamers will work fine with your tenkara rod. If you are new to fly-fishing you will be pleased to know you will not need to learn about entomology, latin, or biological life-cycles of bugs in order to catch fish. Tenkara will show you how.

There are traditional tenkara flies. We don't classify them as dries, wets, or nymphs; they are simply tenkara flies. Tenkara flies are suggestive of many bugs rather than imitative of particular insects, which makes them very versatile. Their versatility shows in the approach taken by experienced tenkara anglers who don't change flies to match insects but rather focus on their technique. "Any fly is okay," as you will learn in this book.

The Japanese term for flies is *kebari*, which literally means "haired hook." Kebari is the word most people in the tenkara community have adopted and use regularly to refer to tenkara flies, especially the reverse-hackle (*sakasa*) style commonly used in tenkara.

Tenkara flies can look different from the western flies and often have their hackle pointing away from the bend of the hook. The reverse hackle allows us to impart motion onto the flies, which is a big benefit of the kebari.

The tenkara fly, in its simplicity and versatility, shows us there is a different way of thinking about fly-fishing.

You will learn more about tenkara flies on page 89

Tenkara: The Method v. The Tool

Some people may interpret tenkara as meaning the tool, that is, a portable telescopic tenkara rod with line tied to the end. Those who look at tenkara simply as a tool will attempt to use this rod, line, and fly with other techniques known to them. "Is tenkara dry-fly fishing?" or "is tenkara just like high-stick nymphing?" they will ask.

The reality is that tenkara is its own complete method of fishing. It has its own history, equipment, flies, and also techniques. It is a style of fishing all in its own right.

This is the first book on tenkara that covers tenkara from a pure tenkara point of view, as it is practiced in Japan. This book takes into account centuries of learned techniques and the refinements that have taken place over time to give us simple and effective tackle and technique. What I cover here is the method as a whole, not just the tools.

There is nothing wrong with using tenkara as a tool. If you already come from a western fly-fishing background your tenkara rod can be paired with a variety of techniques. People have used the long reach of tenkara rods for European nymphing techniques. Anglers also enjoy the use of tenkara for great presentations of dry flies.

But, I believe looking at tenkara simply as a tool is the quickest way to complicate fly-fishing and not take advantage of the benefits of tenkara. For example, using a PVC floating line means that the angler will end up with line on the water that will be dragged by the currents between him and the fly, negating one of the main advantages of tenkara: the ability to cast light lines that can be kept off the water. Additionally, doing so would require carrying leaders and different lines depending on what the angler intends to accomplish.

This book covers the method as a whole. It gives you the tools and knowledge to keep fly-fishing simple and effective.

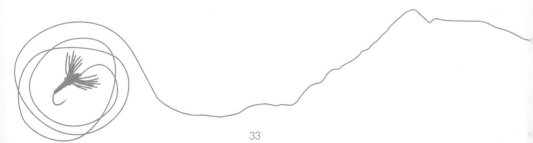

The *Fuji no Hana* drapes over a river in Japan indicating the tenkara season has started.

The Tenkara Flower

It was May 25, 2010, exactly one year after I last fished with Dr. Ishigaki and he had adopted me as his "tenkara son" when I saw him again. He had told me to come fish with him in Japan and I booked a flight as soon as I could.

We met at the Nagoya train station and from there he drove my old friend Chikara and me to the mountains of Gifu prefecture. In the mountains it looked like tunnels had been purposefully adorned with violet vines dangling above. When we drove on bridges the rivers below were equally decorated.

The following day I was fishing with Dr. Ishigaki when we saw the lavender color vines and I asked him what they were. That was the *Fuji no Hana* (藤花, fuji flower, *wisteria japonica*), he told me. He explained that it is considered to be the "tenkara flower" as its bloom is a good indication that fishing season has arrived.

The flowers' blossoming starts in southern Japan and in lower lands closer to the coast and then moves northward and into the mountains. Late May and June are often considered the best time for tenkara fishing in the mountain streams of Japan, particularly in the Japanese Alps. The flower's blossom likely correlates to increased bug activity. It also coincides with the slower flow in rivers as the runoff from snowmelt comes to an end. I always look forward to its sight when visiting Japan at that time of year.

Where to Try Tenkara

Tenkara can be used in a variety of waters: mountain streams, large rivers, hop-across brooks, slow spring creeks, and even lakes. However, it must be noted that tenkara originated in mountain streams and rivers.

Moving water, mountain streams in particular, is where tenkara truly shines. Moving water, with currents ready to quickly drag line downstream and small pools unwilling to hold lures for long can be challenging to fish. There is no better way to fish mountain streams and rivers than using tenkara.

Mountain streams are a unique type of water to fish and provide the opportunity to learn a lot about fishing techniques that can be applied to different types of waters.

There is great diversity among mountain streams in Japan and elsewhere; some are large and others small, some are slow and meandering, others are fast and tumbling. The one thing they all have in common is moving water. And, often times they will have a variety of distinct features such as boulders cropping out of the water, areas where fast water meets slow water, undercut banks, foam lines and sometimes even currents that go upstream rather than down. Because of this variety of conditions, I believe if one learns how to fish a mountain stream, one can fish anywhere.

Because mountain streams provide such an opportunity to learn, and also because that's where tenkara originated and where I have spent most of my time learning tenkara, mountain streams will be the focus of this book.

Some traditionalist tenkara anglers in Japan will point out that what we know as tenkara is what is done in mountain streams and nowhere else. While I agree that tenkara looks most like tenkara when done in a mountain stream, in my opinion the waters where it is practiced do not define tenkara. Tenkara can be used in a large river just the same as it can be used in a small creek. As some people will point out, a large river is really a series of small streams next to each other. People can also use tenkara in lakes, which, after all can be like the occasional deep pool found within mountain streams.

History

The best way to understand tenkara is to know its history. Although we now use modern materials for our equipment, the essence of tenkara remains virtually unchanged from when it started. While there are uncertainties regarding the earliest origins of tenkara, of one thing we can be certain: tenkara was historically the method of fishing practiced by professional fishermen in the mountain streams of Japan.

It is thought that mountain folk devised the method of fly-fishing we know as tenkara approximately 500–600 years ago. The estimate of when tenkara came about is admittedly not much more than an educated guess. There are no ancient records of tenkara, and any early tackle—probably made of organic material such bamboo rods, silk or horsehair lines, and flies made with feathers—has long ago disintegrated.

While there are several theories as to the origins of tenkara, with people speculating that it could have been brought to Japan from other cultures, I believe tenkara originated independently in the hands of mountain folks who needed to catch the local resource for a living. Assuming otherwise greatly underestimates the creativity and ingenuity of native peoples.

It is easy to picture a mountain person noticing fish feeding on bugs fluttering about on the water. The mountain person would then have tried to figure out how to catch that fish. To attract the fish, he would need bait, and the bugs on which the fish were feeding would work well. Unlike other methods used by commercial anglers, nets would be useless in fast-flowing mountain streams with lots of places for fish to hide. Eventually, tired of losing the bugs he had worked hard to capture and which were lost every time he missed a bite, the mountain angler would look at his fraying pants and at a feather he found earlier and think, "Why not make a fake bug?"

Something sharp, a needle perhaps, would be bent to use as hook. Silk and horsehair proved to be great materials for making lines. The lines would be relatively heavy to begin with to ensure they didn't break easily. And, when faced with the challenge of getting the crude fly a little farther out, the fisherman would intuitively begin casting—swinging his pole to make the fly move forward. This way, the trout was fooled by a fly and the native person became a fly-fisherman, a tenkara angler. The method was then passed from one generation to another.

Commercial anglers in Japan

Dr. Hisao Ishigaki reenacts a commercial tenkara angler for a Japanese TV show in the 1980s.

Mr. Ernest Satow

A couple of *iwana* in a clear
mountain stream in Japan

The First Account of Tenkara

Tenkara's recorded history is spotty, largely due to the fact that it was a method of fishing practiced by illiterate anglers more interested in securing food than writing about it. Whereas we have numerous ancient records of western fly-fishing, it took hundreds of years for the first record of tenkara to appear.

The most widely accepted first record of tenkara is from 1878, penned by Sir Ernest M. Satow, a British diplomat who spent a large part of his career (from 1862 and 1883) in Japan. Mr. Satow was a keen mountaineer with a sense of adventure and a yearning to explore the farther reaches of Japan, the places where tenkara would have been practiced. In his diaries we can find numerous passages that describe his encounter with tenkara, though none of them explicitly say "tenkara," a term that only became popular in the 1970s.

On multiple occasions Mr. Satow describes visiting the mountains now known as the Japanese Alps. Areas known for cold streams, abundant trout, and a thriving tenkara community are featured prominently in his writings, in particular Mt. Tate (Tateyama) and Mt. Ontake (Ontake-san).

On September 22, 1877, Mr. Satow wrote about his time near the river Katashina-gawa (gawa = river): "Bears, deer, wild boar & hare taken in the winter months; yamame (trout) with artificial flies."

Then, during a period of about 10 days in 1878, Mr. Satow described his voyage in the Japanese Alps, writing three passages relevant to tenkara:

July 23 1878: "...Height about 7500 or 8000 ft... Below the top large yellow ranunculus 3 & black lilies in abundance 4; then rhododendrons in flower... Magnificent rocky cliffs tower above us all the way to the first hut at Futamata, then the sides of the ravine slope more, and are generally covered with trees. The ice cold stream boils along over rocks of grey granite, & so cold is it that in crossing one bridge we actually feel the consequent change of temperature."

July 24, 1878: "Last night we had for dinner capital fish called iwana [a native Japanese trout], caught in the Kurobe-gawa with a fly made of cock's feathers, weighing about 3/4 lbs."

July 28, 1878: "Our coolies were provided with bamboo rods and flies to fish for iwana in a stream near Kamidaki."

テンカラ

The Commercial Angler

The original tenkara anglers were commercial fishermen who, from perhaps the 15th century until the last known of them retired in the 1950s, caught fish with flies for a living. Yet, out of necessity, they had to keep their gear incredibly simple and rely more on technique than on gadgets.

I like to think of the original tenkara anglers in order to understand tenkara. This helps me realize that fly-fishing really is that simple, and that nothing but the essential is necessary to catch fish.

The original tenkara anglers did not go after trout for fun or sport. Rather, they practiced tenkara as a means of securing food for themselves and their village. Some tenkara anglers would walk to streams for a day, catch fish and then sell their catch to neighbors and innkeepers. Others would disappear into the forests for weeks at a time. They would claim a piece of river, build a hut they could return to, and proceed to fish there for a period of time. They would dry most of the fish they caught, and when it looked like one more fish would make the load too heavy, they headed back to their village in order to sell the product of their labor.

They were very poor, and thus could not afford to use anything that was not absolutely necessary. They had to be pragmatic and rely on simple tools and on their experience and techniques.

These were some of the most effective stream anglers the world has ever known. One hundred–fish days were common, and two hundred–fish days happened with relative frequency according to some of the late commercial anglers.

Fortunately the knowledge acquired by the original tenkara anglers wasn't completely lost to time. It has survived by being passed on to new generations of tenkara anglers, even if it had to be "stolen" by the newer generations.

I like to think that knowledge will live on through this book.

10kara.co/8

Read the story of the last commercial tenkara angler, Bunpei Sonehara

Tenkara As a Sport

For centuries tenkara was practiced in Japan as a means of securing food. When it was no longer necessary (due to the creation of fish farms) or feasible (due to the damming of rivers and reduced fish stock in streams) to catch mountain trout for a living, the method survived in the hands of a few who continued enjoying it partially as a sport and partially to bring a couple of fresh fish home.

Only when leisure for leisure's sake started becoming accepted by society in Japan did tenkara start enjoying relative popularity as a bona-fide sport. In the 1970s, Mr. Yamamoto Soseki, who learned tenkara under Dr. Hideki Sugimoto, wrote the first comprehensive book about tenkara, *Mountain Fishing in Western Japan*. Mr. Soseki is now known as the "father of modern tenkara," and he introduced a whole generation to an activity they could enjoy as a sport. Following Mr. Soseki, in the early 1980s, a few tenkara enthusiasts, among them my teacher Dr. Ishigaki, started spreading the method throughout Japan via videos, articles, and television.

Dr. Hisao Ishigaki, in particular, can be seen as the elemental force in both bringing together a vast body of knowledge about tenkara as well as spreading the method throughout Japan. As he tells me, in the late 1970s mountain streams started attracting him and he became interested in fishing them. At first he tried going out with lures but did not have much success. In one of his outings, he noticed someone using tenkara and catching fish, so he decided to find some information and try that method instead. In his first couple of outings he didn't catch a single fish, but he knew that it was not because of the equipment; after all he had just seen someone catching fish with tenkara. Rather, he knew it was just a matter of acquiring the technique.

There was little information he could find in books or magazines about the method he had witnessed, and he didn't know anyone at the time who could teach him. Being a scholar (Dr. Ishigaki earned his doctorate in the field of vision studies and is a professor at the Aichi Institute of Technology), he decided to do some experiments to try uncovering some of the mysteries of fooling trout with a fly. He did a series of articles for *Tsuribito*, the largest fishing magazine in Japan. The articles covered topics ranging from what it is that trout could see to how fast they would spit out a fly that they had taken in their mouth.

The magazine started getting correspondence from people who knew tenkara. These were people who had learned it from their parents or neighbors. This was the first time tenkara got any widespread attention in Japan, and it was also the first time tenkara anglers from different parts of the country started communicating with one another. What was seemingly kept as a secret was now becoming known.

The articles, books on tenkara, and meeting of tenkara enthusiasts ensured tenkara was not lost to time. In fact, tenkara started spreading throughout Japan as a fun sport.

Fishing is very popular in Japan. Most people who visit Japan will see a number of anglers throughout the country. Some of these anglers will be fishing large rivers and can be seen right from the windows of the fast *shinkanzen* trains and will be using very long telescopic rods. In and near cities, there is a good chance of seeing folks using telescopic rods for catching carp or minute telescopic rods for catching tanago. In the mountains of Japan, visitors will see anglers using telescopic rods with bait, in what is called the *keiryu* fishing method to catch trout. To the unaccustomed eye, all these methods share some resemblance to tenkara in that they are using long telescopic rods with lines tied to the end. But they should not be confused; each method is very distinct, with its own techniques and gear.

Visitors to Japan will also see people using spinning reels with lures and even anglers using a fly rod and reel and wearing the traditional multi-pocketed vest. But, I can say most visitors will likely not see tenkara anglers on a casual visit to Japan. Tenkara is not the most popular method of fishing in Japan (bait fishing is still king there). And, the majority of tenkara anglers will be seek solitude and will head deeper into the mountains.

Yes, tenkara is alive and well in Japan. But, at this point tenkara has already become bigger outside its country of origin. And, paradoxically the introduction of tenkara outside of Japan is now contributing to wider adoption of tenkara there too!

There is a term in Japanese, *Gyakuyunyu*, which means "reimportation," and refers to the fact that sometimes a product, brand, or concept from Japan becomes popular in other countries and suddenly there is a renewed interest in Japan too. This is often mentioned to me when I visit. When I introduced tenkara to the world, I had no idea Japanese anglers would one day attribute its growing popularity to my efforts outside of Japan.

Japanese tenkara anglers have expressed great pride that this method is gaining acceptance abroad. Now, a younger generation is rediscovering the merits of the method created by their forefathers. They too are learning that fly-fishing does not have to be complicated.

The Link Between Ancient and Modern Tenkara

Yoshimaru Shotaro estimates he started tenkara fishing in 1938 at age 12. At that time, there were no teachers around. One summer afternoon Shotaro-san noticed an angler catching fish in a stream near his home in Hagiwara, Gifu prefecture.

For the rest of summer, he followed the tenkara angler from a distance, trying not to be noticed as he observed the angler's techniques. After watching for a bit, he would try to copy what he saw. Mr. Shotaro said, "I stole his techniques."

Until this point tenkara had been practiced by commercial anglers who caught fish for a living. They would not share their techniques with others for fear of having more competition for the fish they were targeting.

After teaching himself tenkara for a few years, Shotaro-san started teaching tenkara to people in his town, first to friends, then to people at an informal fishing club that he helped start. A master, by definition, is someone who "becomes an expert at a skill and shares it with others." Mr. Shotaro was one of the early tenkara masters, someone who not only became an expert in tenkara but also shared what he knew.

Shotaro-san stopped fishing about three years before I met him in 2011. He felt that his legs could no longer safely support him in the stream. He clearly missed his favorite pastime. However, after we chatted about fishing for a couple of hours, Shotaro-san got excited. I saw a spark in his eye at the exact moment he decided to fish again. Through my friend Osaki-san, who was translating for us, Mr. Shotaro said he wanted to fish with me.

He asked for help putting on waders. Along with one of his students, we slowly proceeded to the Mazegawa river in front of the fishing center where I had been spending the summer. We arrived at the water, and he proceeded to cast his fly to the middle of a run. He used a wading staff for extra support and with his right hand worked on bringing the tenkara fly to life by pulsating it rhythmically.

The stretch of river we fished didn't have many fish but he still managed to get two fish to chase his fly in our short time out. When I asked him why was it that people today thought fishing was difficult, even with all the books, videos and instructors available, his response was simple: "There were more fish back then."

Mr. Shotaro and a student fishing on the Mazegawa in Japan.

Philosophy

It has been said that if you give someone a fishing rod, he will instantly become a philosopher. I am no different. I have gathered two guiding principles about tenkara: the concept of simplicity and the focus on technique rather than gear. These principles are interconnected. Choosing to rely on technique more than on gear means you can leave the unnecessary behind and keep things simple. And, when we decide to simplify and leave things behind, we are put in a position of learning how to use what we have and relying on technique rather than additional gear.

It is worth noting that tenkara's simplicity wouldn't mean much it if weren't also for its effectiveness. In 1890, the British Japanologist Basil Hall Chamberlain remarked in his book *Things Japanese*: "To an English eye the native method of fly-fishing will be rude; but it is justified by its results." I like to think "rude" is another word for simplicity here. It is undeniable that tenkara produces results.

It is often said that tenkara teaches people to fish, rather than to use gear. I have found this to be very true. When we have fewer pieces of equipment to focus on, we are free to pay attention to form, technique, and the environment around us rather than the line wrapped around our legs or the reel that locked up.

Simplicity
Simplicity can mean a lot of different things: minimalism, accessibility, ease, fewer moving parts, clean design, and so forth. Tenkara can embody several of those meanings.

Partly inspired by his tenkara practice, Ryan Jordan, founder of Backpacking Light, breaks simplicity into two distinct types:

> *Practical simplicity is that type of simplicity where I crave not having to fool around with anything, and where everything is just plain easy and effective.*

> *And then there is natural simplicity—that type of simplicity where the process brings you more in touch with the natural world, thus becoming less about the gear and more about the experience.*

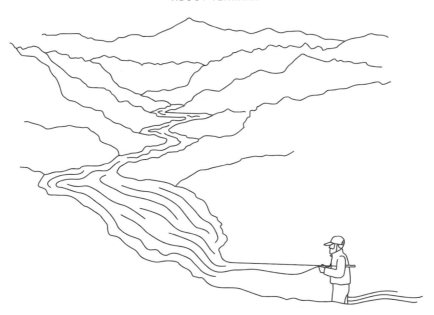

The combination of the practical and the natural simplicities is what makes tenkara a very elegant and effective way to fish. It is also what makes tenkara feel like a relaxing and unencumbered experience.

It is important not to think of tenkara's simplicity in terms of lacking in things to learn, lacking nuance, or being "simplistic." Yes, tenkara eliminates the complexities that don't add to the experience but it does not eliminate the need to learn.

> *For the simplicity on this side of complexity, I wouldn't give you a fig. But for the simplicity on the other side of complexity, for that I would give you anything I have.* — Oliver Wendell Holmes

I'd argue tenkara is one of those things we can say is very easy and simple to learn but can take a lifetime to master. The pages that fill this book will offer the nuanced knowledge needed to master tenkara. A lot of it is instinctive and just waiting to be activated.

I have come to believe that the best way to keep fly-fishing simple is to look at how the Japanese anglers practice tenkara and learn from them. They are truly masters of simplicity. From using one knot for every part of their rig to keeping their fly choices to a minimum (often one!) to not carrying a bunch of accessories and not having to consult hatch charts, the Japanese anglers have kept fly-fishing simple, and because of that we can as well.

We must be aware that simplicity is also the buzzword of today's complicated world. Unfortunately "simple" can be deemed meaningless when it is so often used to describe something that is not actually simple. Simple fly-fishing is not so simple when we choose to keep it complicated by using multiple fly patterns, unnecessary elements in our rig, needless casting techniques or equipment that must to be changed depending on conditions.

Simplicity is a choice. It is easy to make many things in life complex, but these complexities don't usually add to our experience. Even when we learn that we don't truly need a lot of flies we can choose to carry multiple fly patterns with us "just in case". We can carry multiple line weights and change them any time winds change. We can carry accessories to indicate the presence of fish when we could have kept an eye to line to do that. It may seem like carrying additional items in our fishing kit will make fishing easier or more effective. Often it does not.

Two things will help simplify fly-fishing. First, think back to what the commercial angler would have used to catch fish and ask what you truly need in your kit. Second, know that versatility breeds simplicity. When the angler ties a floating line to the tip of her rod, that line will do one thing well: float. Then, if a deeper presentation is necessary she will be forced to change lines or not fish where she wanted. When an angler has a fly that imitates a pale morning dun, he may feel forced to change when he sees a caddis fluttering around.

On the other hand, a lightweight but sinking tenkara line can be kept off the water for presentations on the surface or it can be lowered into the water for a presentation a few feet below the surface. Thus, just one line needs to be used. And a suggestive fly and good presentation will work as well when the mayfly breaks the water's surface as when a caddis skates across it.

Tenkara shows us there is a different way of thinking about fly-fishing – and often about life too. It shows us we can leave the unnecessary behind. But, we must choose to do so.

This book should take you to the simplicity on "the other side of complexity," that which is unencumbered but produces results.

The More You Know the Less You Need

My grandfather used to say, "Knowledge is the only thing no one can take away from you." The nicest thing about knowing is that once you know you can leave a lot of things behind. And, as they say, "Knowledge is weightless."

If you know that you can keep the line off the water to fish near the surface or that fish will also take submerged flies, you don't need...floatant.

If you know how to use currents to sink your fly, then you don't need...split shot.

If you know how to keep your line tight and watch it carefully for subtle hints of fish below the surface, then you don't need...strike indicators.

If you know how to tie a couple of simple knots, then you don't need...tippet rings.

If you know 5X and 6X look virtually the same underwater, then you don't need...multiple spools of tippet.

If you know most fish will be caught between 15 and 40 feet away from you, then you don't need...a bunch of line.

If you know tenkara allows you to keep your line off the water, then you don't need...to mend.

If you know how to tie flies by holding the hook, then you don't need...a vise.

If you know most artificial flies resemble many different things under water and that you can present one fly in different ways, then you don't need...30 fly patterns.

If you know the points above, you don't need...a vest full of pockets.

If you know you can fish with a fixed-length of line...and,

If you know you can land a fish without a reel, you don't need...a reel.

Kirby Wilson of Fresh Catch Gyotaku captures the joy of tenkara in this photo of his son.

Kirby Wilson

Have Fun Fishing Like a Child

It seems to me that children have an easier time than adults just having fun for fun's sake. There is a kind of joy I see in kids' faces when they fish, and it reminds me of my own experiences fishing as a child. I admit sometimes I am jealous of that unfiltered fun.

Some talk of tenkara as "fishing for children," as if to imply it is a lower form of fishing that's only exciting for the young.

My friend Eiji Yamakawa, who's been tenkara fishing for decades responds: "'Fishing for children' is a great compliment to me. I usually wish to enjoy fishing like a child, being free from the constraints of the world. We used to fish by very simple tackle—a pole, line, bobber, sinker, hook, and worm—when we were children, and that was very fun. I liked to fish by a very simple tackle like a child, and it is tenkara for me now. The simpler the tackle and the technique, the more enjoyable the fishing is. Enjoy fishing like a child."

Many people have dismissed tenkara as "just cane-pole fishing." I take no offense to this since the cane-pole fishing I did as a kid was tremendously fun. I always like to think of tenkara as the perfect marriage of the simplicity of the cane-pole fishing I did as a kid with the elegance of fly-fishing I came to learn over the years. The simple type of fishing from my childhood and the joyful fun I experienced on Sunday afternoons catching panfish is what sparked my love for the sport of finding and catching fish.

Tenkara USA
The introduction of tenkara outside of Japan

I was not the first person to see tenkara being practiced in Japan and I was not the first Westerner to fish with a tenkara rod. But, for whatever reason tenkara had not found its way outside of Japan in any meaningful way.

When tenkara came into my life, it inspired me and I started sharing its simplicity with friends. I realized this simpler way to fish could open the doors to fly-fishing for a multitude of people. I wanted to share tenkara with the world.

I have always been passionate about sharing things I like with others. If people could see that fly-fishing did not have to be complicated, I believed they would also enjoy using fly-fishing as an excuse to go outside.

The first thing that crossed my mind when I held the telescopic rod in Japan was that it would be the perfect backpacking rod. So, from the beginning I wanted to share the tools of tenkara with those interested in fly-fishing while backpacking or partaking other outdoor activities, such as hiking, climbing, canyoneering, and cycling.

The first two friends who I told about tenkara upon returning from my first visit to Japan were never interested in fishing but were avid backpackers. They became intrigued when I told them about the portable tenkara rods. I decided the best way to share the tenkara story would be to put tenkara rods in people's hands. And, so I set off to work for several long months on developing Tenkara USA and the equipment needed to fish with tenkara. I was investing my personal savings and taking a gamble by leaving a promising career in international banking to start a company promoting a foreign method of fishing that very few people had heard of.

As John Gierach later wrote in his book *All Fisherman are Liars*, "[Daniel is] not unaware of the difficulties of introducing something small, quiet and simple to a country that likes things big, loud and complicated."

On April 12, 2009 Tenkara USA went live on the web. We sold our first rod that same day and that marked the official introduction of tenkara to the world. Since then, Tenkara USA has helped people discover a more accessible way to fly-fish. It has opened doors for the adventurer interested in fishing while in the backcountry. And, it has showed the experienced angler there is a different way of thinking about fly-fishing, a simple way to fly-fish.

Over 400 years ago, tenkara is developed by commercial anglers in the mountain stream of Japan as a way to catch trout for a living.

In the 1970's **Mr. Yamamoto Soseki** starts writing about tenkara and introduces a new generation of Japanese anglers to a forgotten sport.

In the 1980's **Dr. Hisao Ishigaki** researches traditional tenkara techniques and with his friends starts spreading tenkara in Japan.

Check out Tenkara USA's interactive timeline

Ernest Satow, a British diplomat climbing Mt. Tateyama in Japan observes people catching iwana with long rods and artificial flies and writes about in his diary.

In 2009, **Daniel Galhardo** starts Tenkara USA and introduces people outside of Japan to a simpler way to fly-fish.

TENKARA+

Tenkara fishing is very simple, which makes me feel I am a part of the mountains.
If you want to submerge yourself deep in nature, it is the best fishing style.
But just through the act of fishing, we won't be able to enjoy the real thrill and joy
of tenkara fishing. Fishing becomes much more fun by experiencing the joy of
being able to be a part of nature and learning something new in nature.
YUZO SEBATA

In addition to showing people that fly-fishing does not have to be complicated, I also want to tell people that fly-fishing and other activities are not mutually exclusive. In 2013 I released the campaign I called TENKARA+, which is the idea that you can do tenkara plus anything.

For years I felt I had to choose between activities to enjoy on my free days. It was either rock climbing or fishing. It was either mountain-biking or fishing. It is always too difficult to choose between things one loves. Luckily, tenkara with its minimal amount of gear and the ease of its setup showed me it doesn't have to be one or the other. Of course, I could continue enjoying a full day or several days of fishing, but I could start bringing tenkara along anywhere I went just in case I had the opportunity to fish.

As fly-fishing author Dave Hughes writes in his book *Trout from Small Streams, 2nd edition,* "Tenkara fishing can be an end in itself, but it's also an excellent adjunct to a day hike, backpacking trip, berry picking expedition, or any other activity that gets you out in the world where you might come across a trout stream."

To the rock climber, backpacker, mountain biker, mushroom hunter, surfer, hiker, canyoneer, and other adventurers out there, just know that you can always bring tenkara along.

Along hiking trails there will often be streams, rivers and lakes. A climber may initially see the stream as a nuisance, an obstacle to be crossed. But, knowing he can fish it for a few minutes if a trout reveals itself can turn the stream from a nuisance into a new part of the playground.

These days, rather than going out exclusively for fishing an entire day, more often than not I will go walk my dog, look for edible mushrooms, climb cliffs and bring a tenkara rod along so that I can pull it out when I want to fish for a moment.

Daniel goes in search of tenkara at the bottom of Freemont Canyon, WY.

Jeffrey Rueppel

part
two

equipment

Standard Setup

12 foot rod, 12 foot line, 4 feet of 5X tippet, size 12 fly

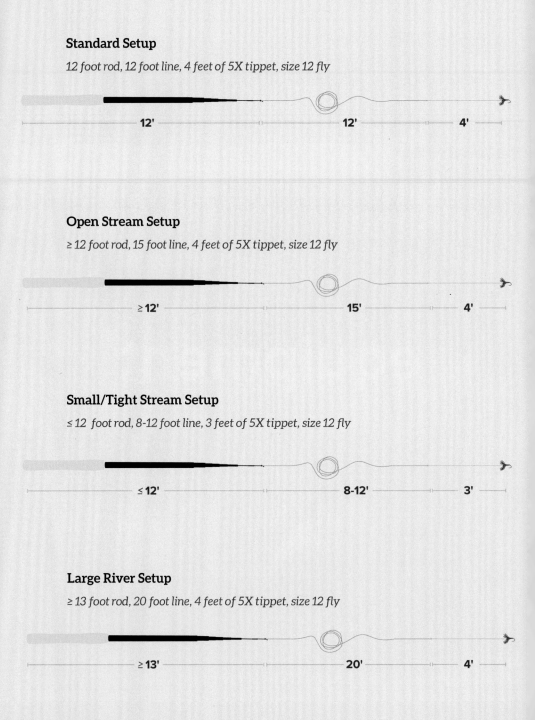

12'   12'   4'

Open Stream Setup

≥ 12 foot rod, 15 foot line, 4 feet of 5X tippet, size 12 fly

≥12'   15'   4'

Small/Tight Stream Setup

≤ 12 foot rod, 8-12 foot line, 3 feet of 5X tippet, size 12 fly

≤12'   8-12'   3'

Large River Setup

≥ 13 foot rod, 20 foot line, 4 feet of 5X tippet, size 12 fly

≥13'   20'   4'

The Complete Setup

The basic rig used in tenkara consists of a rod, line about the length of rod, some tippet, and fly. As tenkara rods are on average 12 feet long, Jason Sparks came up with what he calls the rule of 12s for the novice tenkara angler: a 12-foot rod, 12 feet of line [plus 4 feet of tippet], and a size 12 fly.

Keep it simple: 12 foot rod, 12 foot line, 4 feet of 5X tippet, size 12 fly

Then, with something more specific in mind, one can start experimenting with lines that are longer or shorter than the rod as one acquires more experience and sees a need to vary. If one if fishing tighter waters then a shorter rod (not much shorter than 10 feet long) will make sense. Also, one could use a line that is a couple of feet shorter than the rod to fish tighter streams. If fishing bigger rivers, then I recommend trying longer lines, adding about 3 feet of line at a time, up to about 1 ½ times the length of the rod.

There are no exact formulas here, as everyone may do it a bit differently. In the following pages I'll cover the range of options you have for rods, lines, and flies.

My Kit

Admittedly, "Only a rod, line & fly" may be oversimplifying things slightly.

The line portion is more accurately described as line and tippet. I also find that forceps to remove hooks that are lodged deeper in a fish, nippers to cut tippet, and a line keeper to manage my line are essential in my kit.

My entire kit is composed of a rod, which I will choose depending on where I am fishing, and a small pouch that contains:

- a small fly box
- a line keeper with two different lengths of line
- a spool of 5X tippet
- forceps
- nippers
- fishing license

I also wear polarized sunglasses, which I always have with me whether I am fishing or not. For me polarized sunglasses are indispensable. They work like x-ray vision and allow anglers to see through the glare in the water to spot fish or identify where fish are likely to hold. Sunglasses also protect the angler's eyes in case a rogue fly comes at them.

If I am going on a dedicated fishing trip, then I may use a few things that make life more comfortable:

10kara.co/10

WADING SAFETY

- a fishing net to help me handle and photograph fish
- waders and wading boots

I leave these behind almost as often as I use them. If I am going on a back-packing trip, I forego my fishing net. If it's hot out, I may not use waders. If you want to wear waders, do look up "wading safety" before you go fishing.

If I'm going out for a few hours of fishing, I may expand my kit to include:

- a small portable water filter

A small water filter allows for a drink directly from the stream. This way I won't run out of water; and a filter is often much smaller than a water bottle.

- a whistle

I started carrying a whistle with me when I read in the news that an angler near Salt Lake City got his foot trapped between two boulders in the water. Unable to free himself and with the loud roar of the stream muffling his calls for help, he spent a cold night in the water until someone spotted him the next morning, alive but very hypothermic. The same evening he got trapped I was fishing the next stream over the mountain just a few miles away.

If I'll be wandering deep into a forested area and there is any remote chance I could get lost I'll also carry:

- a small zip lock bag with a fire-starting sparker and lint

In the following pages, I'll get into details about each of the items that are essential to tenkara: rod, line, tippet, fly, and accessories to manage the line. I'll also introduce you to tenkara nets, which are very useful and a beautiful craft.

Tenkara Rods

Keep it simple: get a rod that covers the 12 foot length, such as the adjustable Tenkara USA Sato, or the Iwana.

Overview

Originally tenkara rods were made of bamboo, a material that was readily available to anglers in Japan. While the essence of a tenkara rod hasn't changed that much, today's tenkara rods are a vast improvement over the bamboo poles used by anglers of the past.

Tenkara rods come in different lengths and are typically longer and lighter than western fly rods. A typical tenkara rod is made of carbon fiber and is 12 feet in length when extended. They are telescopic and collapse down to a mere 20 inches, and often weigh less than 3 ounces.

There is a top plug on the thinner end of a collapsed rod that keeps all the segments inside the handle. On the end of the handle, there is a screw cap, which can be unscrewed to access segments for maintenance. On the very tip of the rod, there is a short segment of soft, red, hollow braided line called the lillian. This is where the line will be attached.

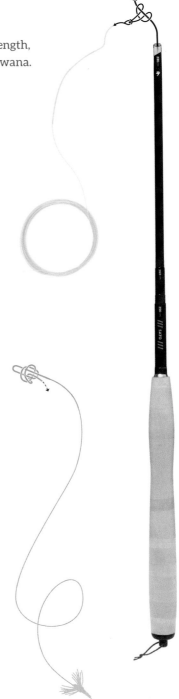

TENKARA
RODS

10kara.co/11

Tenkara rods are designed with four main things in mind:

1 **They must cast a tenkara line well. A tenkara rod works as a whole to propel the tenkara line forward. The tip of the rod must not be too stiff nor to soft, and it must stop oscillating quickly.**

2 **They must be comfortable to cast. One may cast hundreds of times over the course of a day, so tenkara rods must be designed with a comfortable grip and good balance to feel light.**

3 **They must set the hook well. More than a matter of softness/stiffness, the rod as a whole must not have too slow an action; otherwise the delayed hook set will result in missed fish.**

4 **They must play a fish well. A rod should not be too soft, otherwise it will be difficult to control a fish. On the other hand, a rod that is too stiff will not feel great when fighting a fish.**

Let's look at tenkara rods in more detail:

Today's tenkara rods are telescopic. While the extended length of a tenkara rod may be as long as 14 feet, they average about 20 inches when collapsed. Since tenkara uses a fixed line, there is no need for a reel, guides, or reel seats. The segments fit into one another and can be easily removed through the handle for maintenance.

Tenkara rods typically have about 8 or 9 segments. While it would be a nightmare to assemble an 8- or 9-segment reeled fishing rod, with tenkara it is extremely fast and simple. To extend a rod, the angler simply removes the plug, holds the rod at the top opening with two fingers, tilts the rod to expose the tip, and, starting with the tip, pulls one segment out at a time between his fingers until the next one comes out. When fishing, the line is tied to the tip of the rod before the segments are extended (more on that later). The rod is extended much faster than the time it took you to read this paragraph.

The telescopic design of tenkara rods makes them very popular with back-packers and folks looking for a portable fly-fishing solution. I always chuckle when people ask me if I broke my rod when they see me carrying what seems like just the handle of a rod.

How to Choose a Tenkara Rod

Choosing a tenkara rod could feel like the most daunting aspect of tenkara. The advice I usually give is to follow a couple of basic suggestions but to not overthink it. A good tenkara rod should be designed to fish well in a large range of conditions.

The main criteria for choosing your first tenkara rod will be its length, which is primarily dictated by the size of water and amount of overhead coverage you will encounter. Other things to keep in mind are: fish size, quality of materials, features, price, collapsed length, and warranty.

Rod Length

Tenkara rods range in length from just about 9 feet long to just over 14 feet long, with 12 feet being considered the average length and often a good place to start. As I discuss "short" or "long" rods, know that I usually think of rods that are shorter than 11 feet long as short rods, and rods that are 13 feet long or longer as long rods.

> Consider 12 feet to be the middle and good option for a wide range of conditions.

> Look at rods that are about 9 to 11 feet long if you know you will fish very tight streams.

> Consider rods 13 feet long or longer if you're in more open streams with little canopy overhead or if you like to fish larger rivers and lakes.

> Adjustable-length rods are often excellent choices as they cover different lengths and work well in different situations.

The question of what length rod to get is an easy one to get caught up on, but it shouldn't be. Most tenkara rods will work fine in a wide range of conditions, and you will adapt to the tool you choose by using some techniques discussed later in this book or by focusing on the water you are effectively reaching. Rod length is primarily determined by a combination of personal preference and the type of water fished most often, more specifically the type of vegetation around a stream.

My main recommendation is to get the longest rod you can manage for the water you typically fish. Unless you have a very specific need for a rod less than 10 feet long (if you fish places with tight canopy overhead), I suggest the longer options.

As a generalization, when fishing in waters surrounded more by conifers, which stand tall on the sides but not as much over the stream, a longer rod will be fine. When fishing in places with lots of overhanging canopy, such as streams in the Appalachian regions, shorter rods may be more desirable.

Longer rods translate into the ability to reach across multiple currents with no line touching the water—a very desirable aspect of tenkara. The rod you'll find in my hands most often is the Ito, which can be fished at 13 feet or 14 feet, 7 inches. Even in streams considered "small," such as Boulder Creek which is about 20 feet wide in most areas, I often fish the rod at its fully extended length. A longer rod allows anglers to cover a good amount of water without moving as much and to fish difficult seams across the stream or river.

A rod that is too short will frustrate an angler with limited reach, also forcing her to extend the arm, which can be tiring. It may seem counterintuitive, but a longer rod can mean less arm fatigue since it allows you to keep your arm by your side when fishing.

I have found that rods outside the 9- to 15-foot-long range to be impractical. On the shorter end, I have not yet seen a real need for rods that are shorter than 9 feet long (or 8 feet, 10 inches based on the last rod I designed). A tenkara rod of that length is plenty short for the majority of tight areas. And, one can always choke up on the grip by holding the rod about 2 feet above the end, which would bring the effective length of the rod to 7 feet long.

If the stream gets even tighter than that for a moment, then, along with holding the rod 2 feet above the end, one can also collapse the first segment of the rod (which is close to 2 feet long on most rods); this way the effective length of the rod would be a mere 5 feet. I'll discuss some techniques and strategies for tight waters later on.

Rods longer than 15 feet are impractical for the tenkara fishing. The longest rod in our lineup as I write this book is an adjustable rod that can be fished at 13 feet long or 14 feet, 7 inches. Longer rods move the center of balance of a rod away from one's hand and closer to the tip of the rod, making them feel tip-heavy. At 15 feet or so I have found rods are not very pleasant to cast for extended periods of time. Thus, I'd personally stay away from anything longer than 15 feet long being marketed as "tenkara".

Rod Handle

The handle of a tenkara rod serves the very important function of ensuring a comfortable grip while you cast your fly into a stream hundreds of times over the course of a day. Tenkara technique involves quick and frequent casting rather than casting and waiting. It's an active method of fishing. This makes it necessary for the rod to be lightweight and comfortable to use.

The handle of a tenkara rod is designed with comfort in mind, but its ergonomic shape also helps the rod feel balanced and light. There are a variety of handle shapes—some flat, others contoured; some short, others long. After much experimentation, I have determined that the best handles are contoured and relatively long. A longer handle will allow for the rod to be held in different places and for micro adjustments that will feel best in some situations or in the hands of different anglers. A contoured handle drastically helps reduce fatigue.

You can hold the rod anywhere you want; after all, there is no reel telling you where to hold the rod. The position that will give you the most reach and comfort is generally at the very end of the handle. Holding the rod a bit higher up on the handle will help when the stream gets a little tighter and will make the rod feel lighter since you'll be holding it closer to its balance point. On occasion it can be useful to hold it higher up to give yourself a little bit of a rest.

You can hold the tenkara rod handle wherever you want.
Holding it toward the end makes the casting more effortless.
Holding it up higher shortens the rod for tighter waters.

Adjustable Tenkara Rods

Tenkara rods are generally designed to be used at their full extension. However, to offer rods that fish very well in a wider range of conditions, I spent time designing adjustable tenkara rods, which can be fished at different lengths.

Adjustable tenkara rods allow anglers to have the reach of longer rods while also having the option to shorten the rod when things get tight. The versatility of adjustable rods can reduce the number of rods an angler needs, thus simplifying the decision-making process of choosing a rod to purchase or to carry.

Opening a Tenkara Rod

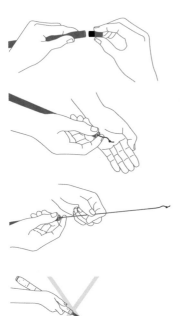

1. Remove the top plug, and tilt the rod slightly to expose the soft braided material. (a.k.a. lillian)

2. To prevent tip breakage, leave hard tip inside the rod (hold it there with one finger to keep it from coming out and snapping), and using the knots suggested on pages 7 & 8, connect your line to the lillian.

3. With one hand holding the rod by the opening and starting with the rod tip, slide each segment out until they become snug with the next segment. Pull all segments out in order.

4. To close the rod, push segments in, always starting with the thickest segment and collapsing them in order. It's best to have the rod parallel to the ground or at a low angle to prevent pieces from sliding in out of order.

Doug Heggart

Jeffrey Rhieppel

Fish Size

Tenkara rods don't have an exact fish-size or weight rating. Much of what they can handle depends on stream currents and the angler's technique. While I don't recommend using tenkara for targeting steelhead, carp, musky, salmon or other large species, all those—as well as a notable 28-inch cutthroat and a 29-inch pike—have been caught with Tenkara USA rods. Most tenkara rods are well-suited for 8- to 20-inch fish, and they can handle the occasional larger fish, too.

If you plan on targeting larger fish species such as bass, or are constantly hooking up with trout over 18 inches, look for rods marketed as "big fish" rods. This is a relative term and subjective, but it will give you an idea that the rod is designed with more backbone to more quickly land larger fish. At the time of this book's publication the 13 foot, 6 inch Amago is the main rod in the Tenkara USA lineup with that designation.

Cost and Warranty

Tenkara rods are available in price points to hit most people's budgets. Some of the price differences can be attributed to features, but the most expensive component of a rod is the carbon fiber used in its construction. Unfortunately carbon fiber quality is not easily distinguished in a finished rod.

TENKARA CARE™

10kara.co/12

The quality of this material is one of the main things that will determine a rod's longevity and breakage rate, and this is one area where typically you get what you pay for.

Also, consider the warranty provided for the rod and how easy it is to get replacement parts. At Tenkara USA we have developed our "Tenkara Care" program, which makes repairing and replacing rod parts painless. In the vast majority of cases, customers never have to mail a broken rod back to us; they simply tell us which segment in their rod broke and we send them a replacement segment. If a breakage happens a customer can be fishing again in as little as 2 days.

ROD CAP

LILLIAN

6 5 4 3 2

TIP-SET
top 3 sections

HANDLE

Keep Your Plug™ system

Since tenkara rods were first invented (including the bamboo predecessors to modern rods), anglers have been cursing the loss of the diminutive components of the tenkara rod. While it's not difficult to find, or even make, a replacement for these plugs, we set out to solve the problem of losing them in the first place.

At the bottom of the rods, where there is a larger screw cap, we have designed a receptacle that will hold the plug while it's not being used. The Keep-Your-Plug™ system is available on select Tenkara USA rods.

Tenkara Rod Plugs

At the top end of a tenkara rod, there is a plug that keeps the rod segments inside the handle. These plugs are an integral part of tenkara rods, yet they are easy to lose. I recommend having a dedicated place to store the plug, such as a specific pocket, so you always know where to find it.

If you lose your plug, one fun option is to carve your own. A custom wooden plug is one of the simplest things to make to add customization and personality to your tenkara gear. Here is Dr. Ishigaki with a plug he carved out of a small twig, and to which he attached a fish carved by a friend.

Examples of Rod Choices by Stream Type

A large river with little cover

GOOD ROD OPTIONS:	PREFERRED TENKARA USA MODELS:
13+ foot long rods	Amago (13'6") & Ito (13'–14'7")

A medium stream with open canopy

GOOD ROD OPTIONS:	PREFERRED TENKARA USA MODELS:
12+ foot long rods	Sato (10'6"–12'9") & Iwana (12') & Ito (13'–14'7")

A small stream with tight cover

GOOD ROD OPTIONS:	PREFERRED TENKARA USA MODELS:
10–12 foot long rods	Rhodo (8'10"–10'6") & Iwana (12')

Our Rod Design Philosophy

The rods we develop are of our own exclusive design but are also guided by the knowledge passed on to me by Japanese tenkara anglers with decades of experience.

The first step in developing a tenkara rod is creating the concept that will be useful to a large number of people. In introducing tenkara outside of Japan I also must take into account the possible differences in how the rods will be used in the US and Europe and the size of fish they will be catching.

The rod must feel very good in the hand and it must be versatile enough to be fished in a wider range of conditions. There are a lot of things that go into developing a good rod, but as I develop the rods I usually keep these main things in mind:

1 **It must feel light on the hand and pleasant to use.** The user will be casting it hundreds of times over the course of a day. A good handle, good balance, and light weight are very important to make a good rod.

2 **It must cast the tenkara line well.** One of the biggest advantages of tenkara stems from the ability to cast super light lines. If a rod is too stiff it won't cast the light tenkara lines well. On the other hand if the rod is too soft throughout its length, it will not make the line move properly. Lastly, if a rod oscillates too much after you shake and stop it, it may be hard to get the line to straighten when you cast.

3 **It must set the hook well.** The rod has to respond quickly and well to set the hook. We are not setting the hook very strongly with tenkara. All it should take to set the hook with a tenkara rod is to tighten the line. If a rod is too soft it won't do that very well. But, a rod that is too stiff on the tip may break tippet.

4 **It must fight and land fish well.** A rod does not have to be classified as a "big fish rod" to bring fish in quickly. Nor does it have to be a very stiff rod to do so. The rod needs to give a bit to protect tippet well but must have a good bounce back to quickly bring fish to hand.

Additionally, as the first company to bring tenkara outside of Japan I knew we would need to create strong durable rods if we were to hope for the introduction of tenkara to be successful. So, I spend a lot of time ensuring that our rods will give anglers confidence in the method and in our brand.

Product Development and Testing

I had my first encounter with Dr. Ishigaki shortly after releasing our first rods. We sat at the Catskills Fly Fishing Center and Museum, and he immediately asked to see the rods I had designed. He went through each of the rods in our lineup, paying attention to minute details in each rod. From that point on Dr. Ishigaki became my mentor and advisor. Each rod gets reviewed by him before it is released.

Margaret Kuwata

Dr. Ishigaki and Daniel review Tenkara USA rods on their first meeting. Catskills, NY, May 2009

On my visits to Japan, I always make sure to schedule time with experienced tenkara anglers and to bring the rods on which I'm working for them to try.

During one trip I scheduled time to fish with Mr. Masami Sakakibara (aka. *tenkara no oni*). Mr. Sakakibara also makes his own brand of high-quality rods, under the *"Oni"* name. On that visit, we rented an old traditional Japanese thatched-roof house near one of his favorite fishing destinations in Nagano prefecture. After a dinner of grilled meat and miso soup we sat down for some fly-tying and wine drinking.

Later in the evening I brought out the prototypes for the rods I had been working on, the *Sato* and *Rhodo*. He then carefully took them apart and looked at each segment while pointing them to the light and explaining how the reflections inside of each segment were good indications of the polish and quality of each segment. Then he put them back together backward to inspect fit. Masami-san nodded at each step of the way. I felt proud at his indications of approval. He particularly liked the clever solution we devised to store the rod plug and advised that I not show it to anyone else until we filed a patent for it; others may want to copy it, he said.

Mr. Yuzo Sebata had helped design a popular tenkara rod for one of the biggest makers in Japan a couple of decades earlier. When I first fished with him, in 2013, he was using the rod he helped design. At the end of our second day, we had some down time by the stream and he asked to cast with the rod I had been using that day, the Ito, which is our longest rod and is an adjustable tenkara rod.

What he really enjoyed about the Ito was its lighter weight. He asked how to get one for himself. As a token of my appreciation I gave him the rod. Upon returning home from my visit to Japan, one of his students contacted me about ordering several rods; each of his closest students wanted one.

Mr. Yuzo Sebata with a native Iwana caught on the Tenkara USA Ito rod.

Hanging out after a long day fishing in Nagano Prefecture in Japan.

Bamboo Tenkara Rods

Originally, tenkara rods were made of bamboo. At first it would have been a thin and long piece of bamboo cut straight out of the ground and immediately used as a fishing pole. Eventually tenkara anglers found ways to make the rods lighter and more portable.

The Japanese rod maker has at his disposal plenty of bamboo from which to choose. He can pick what he wants, selecting the best possible bamboo, straight and thin, just as it comes out of the ground. Unlike western fly rods, which are made from thin strips of a split *Tonkin* bamboo piece, tenkara bamboo rods make use of the natural shape of bamboo and are not split.

A bamboo tenkara rod is typically made of 3 or 4 segments, and each segment is hollowed out. This allows for the sections to be placed inside the thicker ones and make it easy to transport the rod around through the forests.

A few years ago I had the privilege of visiting a family that has been making bamboo tenkara rods for eight generations. I learned that while hobby makers may let the bamboo dry for up to two years, professional makers may let bamboo dry for as long as 10 years before transforming it into a rod.

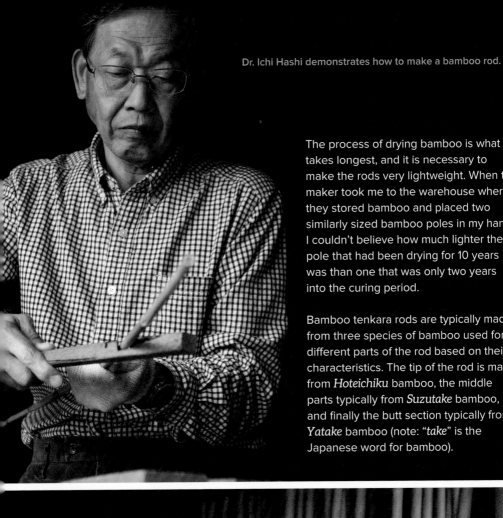

Dr. Ichi Hashi demonstrates how to make a bamboo rod.

The process of drying bamboo is what takes longest, and it is necessary to make the rods very lightweight. When the maker took me to the warehouse where they stored bamboo and placed two similarly sized bamboo poles in my hand, I couldn't believe how much lighter the pole that had been drying for 10 years was than one that was only two years into the curing period.

Bamboo tenkara rods are typically made from three species of bamboo used for different parts of the rod based on their characteristics. The tip of the rod is made from *Hoteichiku* bamboo, the middle parts typically from *Suzutake* bamboo, and finally the butt section typically from *Yatake* bamboo (note: "*take*" is the Japanese word for bamboo).

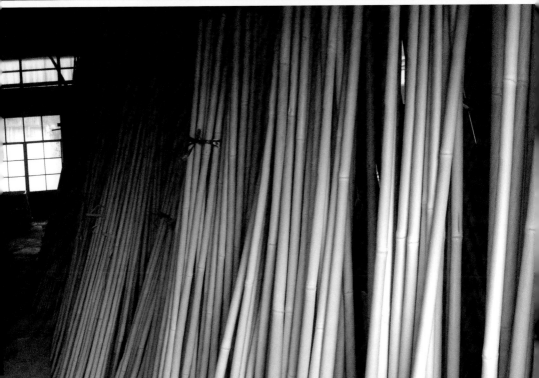

Tenkara Lines

Keep it simple: Start with a tenkara line that is the same length as the rod plus 4 feet of 5X tippet

Overview

The purpose of a tenkara line is to cast the virtually weightless fly. The casting of the line is one of the defining characteristics of fly-fishing and thus tenkara. Tenkara lines are specifically designed for tenkara.

No leader is used in tenkara; at the end of the line, one will use tippet, which is the thin fishing line that goes between the main tenkara line and the fly. Line length will be between 8 feet and 25 feet, and tippet length will be between 3 and 5 feet long.

The main qualities we look for in tenkara lines are the right weight and visibility.

The tenkara line must be heavy enough to cast yet light enough that the line will stay entirely off the water once the fly lands. A line that is too heavy will immediately sag under the rod tip and be picked up by the currents it touches. Very light lines will be more difficult to cast but offer the advantage of staying off the water for a longer distance. A balance between the two is ideal.

The tenkara line must also be very visible so the angler can keep track of it. Line visibility is important to see where the fly landed and will greatly assist in detecting subtle strikes from fish taking the fly underwater. The tenkara line will be a few feet away from the fly, separated by the tippet. The tippet, on the other hand, should be nearly invisible to minimize detection by fish.

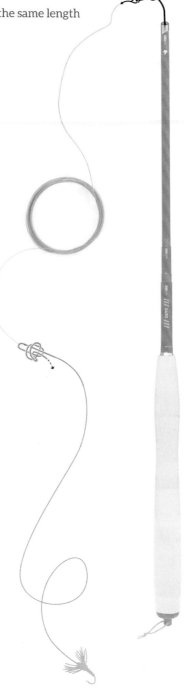

Two concepts I will frequently mention are the idea of "no line touching the water," and "drag." When fishing a stream or river, currents are flowing at different speeds throughout the width of the stream. If line is lying on the water across these currents, the faster current will drag the line faster as the fly stays in slower water. That is called "drag". By keeping line off the water, drag is eliminated. This is one of the hallmark advantages of tenkara.

There are two types of lines that can be used in tenkara: tapered line and level line. Both tapered and level lines have their own characteristics as well as what can be considered pros and cons. However, it should be noted that generally the choice of line has little to do with conditions, situations, or water type and more to do with personal preference.

In Japan I have observed that anglers will use one type of line exclusively. Often an angler will use the same line his teacher uses (even if he only knows the teacher through books), though some anglers will experiment and arrive at their own preference.

Personal preference often comes from the priority given to specific characteristics of the line. For example, some anglers may gravitate toward the tapered line primarily because it casts more easily and softly. Others may lean toward the level line due to its versatility and very light weight.

Since neither line is very expensive, I suggest trying both lines to see which matches your casting style and preferences. However, if you only want to get one type of line to start, I'd recommend a tapered line about the same length as the rod. A tapered line will take but a minute to get used to casting. If you want the flexibility offered by a line that can be cut or joined together, I would recommend the level line. With a level line, you will need to have a faster back-cast (not powerful, just speedier) to make the line move well; it will take just a few minutes to get used to how the line casts.

Floating or Sinking?

Tenkara lines should have a fairly neutral buoyancy or be slowly sinking lines. As it's probably becoming clear by now, tenkara fishing is different from western fly-fishing. We can easily control where the fly will be fished by changing the angle of the rod tip upward or downward. Thus, if we want to fish a fly on or near the surface we just need to keep the rod angled upward and the line off the water. Then, when we wish to sink the fly deeper (sometimes on a second pass in the same pool), we can simply lower the tip of the rod and allow more line to go down following the sinking fly.

If you come from a western fly-fishing background you may be used to floating lines. And while there may be lines marketed for tenkara that are also floating lines, I have stayed away from them and do not recommend them. The main reason is the versatility of a sinking line that allows you to fish with a fly on the surface or deeper without needing to change lines.

Tapered Line

As the name implies, the tenkara tapered line is tapered, starting with a thicker end and becoming thinner as it gets closer to the fly. Tapered lines are either furled (twisted) out of multiple strands of line, or extruded out of a single strand of nylon or other materials. These lines are handmade by the angler or bought at specific lengths.

Originally tapered lines were made out of horse-hair or silk and made by twisting several strands of line together, tapering down from several strands close to the rod tip to fewer strands nearer the fly. Normally a single strand of silk gut was then used as the tippet. Nowadays we can make them out of a variety of materials.

Tenkara tapered lines are not usually marketed in different weights; their main difference will be the length of the line. The angler will choose the length of line based on the streams she's fishing. When fishing tighter streams a line about the same length as the rod will be helpful. In larger and more open streams a line longer than the rod may be desired.

Level Lines

As the name implies, tenkara level lines are of level diameter throughout their length. Level lines come in a spool; and several lines can be cut from the spool at desired lengths.

Tenkara level lines can be considered the more modern version of tenkara lines. They are extruded, meaning they are made into a single filament. Arguably one of the biggest advantages of level lines is that, because of the level-diameter and single-strand construction, they can be cut to whatever length is desired, and if necessary two lines can be joined together.

> **Tip:** Once you cut the desired length of line off a spool you should never have to cut the end of your line to replace tippet. The knot we suggest to tie tippet to your level line will consist of a cinching fisherman's knot that will slide against a small stopper knot at the end of your line. See pages 7 and 8 for the knot we recommend.

Whereas the options available for tapered lines consist mostly of different length options, tenkara level lines are available in different diameters and as a result different weights. The lines we offer at Tenkara USA are designated in half weights: 2.5, 3.5, and 4.5 . The half-weight designation is partly to avoid confusion with western fly lines and partly because I have personally found half weights offer the best range available.

The larger numbers denote heavier lines. A heavier level line will be easier to cast but will sag more under the rod tip. The lighter level line will be easier to keep off the water but may be harder to cast, especially in windy conditions.

The middle weight (3.5) is always a good option and the best way to keep things simple. I use the 3.5 level line nearly exclusively. The 2.5 line can be fun to use and offers great presentations of the fly but is difficult to use in wind. The 4.5 level lines will sag more but come in handy in windy conditions.

Lastly, while most tenkara rods will cast all lines pretty well, the stiffer rods will typically do best with heavier lines. For example, the Tenkara USA Ito, Rhodo, and Sato cast the 2.5 beautifully, so any of the level lines may be used with those. Whereas the Amago, being a heavier rod, does best with a 3.5 or 4.5 line.

Other Lines

Tenkara anglers have experimented with other types of lines ranging from horse-hair to titanium lines to western fly lines. However, none of the other types of lines have gained any traction with anglers in Japan or elsewhere.

And, though I have also experimented with a variety of lines, I personally have found too many drawbacks and little benefit to using other lines for tenkara. For example, using a western fly line will be way too heavy for effective use with tenkara as the line will sag under the rod tip immediately after being cast.

This negates the biggest advantage of tenkara, which is the possibility of using a very light line that stays off the water. Furthermore, the use of a heavy western fly line requires the use of a leader (plus tippet at the end of that). Leaders can be complicated to make, can tangle easily, and will add expense. The tapered and level lines we promote for tenkara offer the best mix of advantages such as light weight, good castability and visibility. Plus, one very important attribute: versatility, where one line can be used to fish in a variety of different conditions, without the need to switch.

Length

A variety of line lengths can be used with tenkara. There is no exact formula to follow. Line lengths can range from a few feet shorter than the rod (useful in very tight waters) to over twice as long as the rod (useful in large rivers), although the tenkara angler can be perfectly happy using the same line wherever he goes.

I typically carry two lines with me when I go fishing: a short line and a long line. If I'm fishing close to home, where the streams are small, I'll take the 12-foot as my short line and a 15-foot line as my long one. If I'm going to a larger river, I'll take a 15-foot line and a 20-foot line. These three lengths give me a very good range.

Short-lining

In very tight streams it is useful to use a line shorter than the rod. The combination of a long rod with a very short line translates into great control of the line and fly with very little rod movement. When things get tight, this combination allows me to cast using a very short flick of my rod tip and keeps me away from trees.

I aim for line plus tippet about 1 or 2 feet shorter than the rod. So, with a 12-foot rod I may use an 8-foot line and 3 feet of tippet. Short-lining can work with any rod length, but I have found it best when used with a tenkara rod that is 12 feet long or longer because short-lining with a very short rod doesn't usually give enough reach.

Long-lining

Tenkara does not mean short-line fishing. Because I love fishing larger mountain streams and rivers I have found knowing how to use a long line to be an important skill and a very fun way to fish with tenkara.

If you fish larger waters and see a need for it, I recommend trying lines progressively longer than the rod. Adding about 3 feet to the main line at a time is a good approach. The main challenge with longer lines will be landing fish, so adding a few feet at a time will allow you to get used to doing that.

Long lines open up our reach considerably and allow for great reach in places that are normally harder to reach for anyone else.

The ability to keep the fly on the other side of currents is one of the main advantages of tenkara.

Effective Reach v. Total Reach

Once I went fishing with a friend who had a good amount of fly-fishing experience but was skeptical of tenkara. He tended to focus on the limitations of tenkara. In particular he was skeptical about having enough reach to get the fly where he wanted. "What if a fish is rising a few feet farther than what I can reach with a tenkara rod and fixed length of line?" he asked.

We went to a relatively large and fast river, the North Fork of the American River in California's Sierra Nevada. I was particularly interested in comparing tenkara to the mending techniques he used to fish that water. I think he was interested in seeing if I could land one of many large browns found there.

After fishing a couple of spots, I asked him to fish a good-looking pocket with a foam line about 30 feet away. The spot was on the other side of some very heavy currents. He told me he couldn't.

> "What do you mean, you can't?" I asked.
> "It's impossible. I can't reach that far," he replied.
> "Don't you have some 50 feet of line in that reel of yours?" I asked.

Despite being a good caster and having plenty of line he didn't try to fish it. He knew the heavy currents would immediately rip his heavy fly line. There was no chance his fly would stay on the calm water long enough to entice a fish. I made the cast, kept the rod tip high and line off the water, and caught a good size rainbow. Then I gave him my rod to try. He liked the reach of the tenkara rod.

Tippet

Keep it simple: 4 feet of 5X nylon tippet

We say in tenkara one uses a rod, line, and fly. More accurate would be to say "rod, line, tippet, and fly". The tippet is the thin fishing line that goes between the main tenkara line and the fly. It helps keep the fly separated from the heavy and more visible main line and allows us to tie the line to the small hook eyes. While some people may use the term "leader" inter-changeably with tippet, we should note that leader is a more specific term in fly-fishing, and in tenkara no leader is needed.

At the end of the tenkara line, regardless of the type or length, attach between 3 and 5 feet of tippet. I typically recommend 4 feet of 5X nylon tippet. I will occasionally use a shorter length of tippet (3 feet) if I'm fishing shallower water with more coverage overhead. If I'm getting a bit of interest from fish but they are rejecting my fly at the last second, or in very clear and calm water, I may go slightly longer and use 5 or so feet of tippet.

Tippet in the US is denoted with the "X" classification (there is a table below). Smaller numbers denote heavier/thicker tippet diameters. I generally recom-mend 5X tippet (roughly equivalent to 5lbs breaking strength). It is plenty thin to not spook fish but strong enough to sustain a bit of abrasion and most fish. If I'm going to be catching a good number of large fish then I may use 4x tippet. But, I don't see a need for other tippet diameters.

Tippet comes in spools with about 90 feet or so, and besides your fly, is the only thing that has to be replaced periodically. Tippet is available in nylon or fluorocarbon materials. Nylon is cheaper and works plenty well; that's what I use. I recommend checking your tippet periodically, especially after freeing a snagged hook, untangling your line or landing a fish. If any section of it feels a bit rough, or if it looks like it may have been damaged, replace it. It's best to replace the tippet than lose it to a fish.

Tippet conversion chart

X	Diameter (mm)	Diameter (inches)	Breaking Strength (kg)	Breaking Strength (lbs)
6X	0.127	0.005	1.5	3.4
5X	0.152	0.006	2.3	5
4X	0.178	0.007	2.9	6.4
3X	0.203	0.008	3.7	8.2

Line Management
Keep it simple: Get a Tenkara USA Keeper (a spool-style line and fly keeper)

There are many different ways to manage line when one is not using it or while you are moving from place to place. I have tested dozens of ways to manage line over the years including techniques developed by anglers in Japan, myself, and other inventors. I will share only my personal preferences here.

If you'll be moving short distances, or through open terrain, it is most efficient to leave the rod extended and wrap the line that goes beyond the length of the rod in large loose coils around your hand. Then poke the fly hook into the rod handle to keep it from hooking you.

> **Tip:** With the line semi-tight make the line spiral around the rod by shaking the rod tip. This will keep the line tight around the rod rather than in a belly under the tip of the rod and will allow you to go through trees you encounter without the line getting snagged along the way.

Wrap the line tight around the rod while moving between largely spaced trees.

A spool, such as the Tenkara USA Keeper, is the best way to keep the line free of tangles and manage line when moving around.

When walking longer distances, or going through trees, brush, or climbing rocks, it is best to collapse the rod. At this point several options are available.

Spools
The most effective way to manage line when moving, as well as to store lines, is to use a spool. Spools not only allow you to manage line while moving, but also give you a place to store line if switching between lines or putting it away. Because they are round, spools will not kink lines around corners.

After trying many different spool systems, we arrived at the design for *The Keeper*, which allows for a couple of lines as well as flies to be stored in one spool and has an innovative way to grab the line. A couple of tips on using spools:

1 **Grab the line with your whole hand,** in your palm, rather than just using a couple of fingers. This will help push any twisting that happens on the lines all the way to the rod tip, which will eventually spin and get rid of line twisting

2 **Hold the spool still with one hand** and use the other hand to wrap line around it (as opposed to the slower way of spinning the spool to get line around it).

3 **Keep your fingers out of the way** of where the line will go.

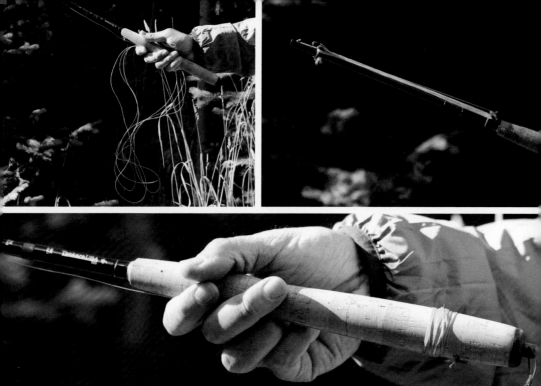

Coiling it loosely on the hand can always be an option. It is quick, you don't need any additional items, and it doesn't create memory but it will often cause the line to tangle.

An "on-the-rod" system allows for a very quick way to manage line . By having two opposing "hooks" on the rod, the angler can wrap line quickly to keep it from tangling as she moves around. Care should be taken not to have the line catch branches when moving.

Unfortunately most of the "on-the-rod" solutions cause kinks on the line, and I have found they take a bit longer to undo when I'm ready to fish. The system I like best that goes on the rod are our Rod Ties, which fit easily on a variety of rod diameters . They are installed quickly and can be positioned wherever the angler prefers. A third tie is handy to secure the fly wherever it stops.

Wrapping it around the rod handle is is probably the simplest option. But the thin rod handle diameter will mean it takes a while to wrap all the line around it, and will cause the line to acquire "memory" in the form of small coils.

Tenkara Flies

Keep it simple: Use a size 12 reverse-hackle tenkara fly.

Overview

Rooted in the origins of tenkara, where simplicity was a result of necessity and effectiveness was mandatory, tenkara flies show us a very different way of thinking about fly-fishing.

Before I go any further, I should note that any fly can be used with tenkara. If you have a favorite go-to fly pattern, continue using it. For the purpose of this book, I will not get into discussions of all the fly types used in western fly-fishing. For those who already fly-fish, I will mention that tenkara rods work well with a variety of flies. Presentation of dry flies is beautiful as the line can be kept off the water and thus there is no drag on the line to make the fly behave unnaturally.

Using nymphs with tenkara is also very effective since the angler will fish with a tight-line. Soft-hackles, terrestrials, and even streamers can be used in tenkara.

One of the most interesting things I have learned from tenkara is the approach taken by tenkara anglers in Japan to their fly selection. Years ago I learned that most experienced tenkara anglers in Japan rely on their one fly pattern and do not change it. This went against anything I had ever read or studied in fly-fishing, but it is one of the main concepts I learned that keeps fly-fishing truly simple.

This book will focus on traditional tenkara flies and the way tenkara anglers approach flies. Unlike most fly-fishing books, this book will not get into discussions about entomology, the study of bugs. While knowing their scientific names and their lifecycles can be fun in its own right, tenkara shows us studying bugs is not fundamental to fly-fishing.

If the idea of using one fly and not having to choose amongst hundreds in a fly-shop's bin is appealing, then you will enjoy learning about the tenkara approach to flies.

Sakasa Kebari

In Japanese an artificial fly is called a *kebari*. *Kebari* literally translates as "haired hook" (*ke* = hair, *bari/hari* = hook). Kebari is the term the tenkara community has largely adopted when referring to tenkara flies in general. To those accustomed to western flies, with their wings and tails and hackle perpendicular or parallel to the hook shank, many tenkara flies will look reversed. Reverse-hackle flies, in Japanese called "*sakasa kebari*," (*sakasa* means reversed in Japanese) are not the only flies used by tenkara anglers, but they are by far the most common.

Reverse-hackle flies may have developed this way for three main reasons: First, they are incredibly easy and quick to tie. With the reverse-hackle fly, one wraps a bit of thread behind the eye of the hook, secures a feather, wraps that feather around, brushes the feather (i.e. hackle) forward and away from where the tier will work next, builds the body with the same thread, and then finishes the fly on the body.

Tenkara was developed for fishing in moving water, which brings us to the second reason reverse-hackle flies may have become popular with tenkara. When the angler casts the fly into moving water, the currents will push the hackle back. The reversed hackle will be brushed back. However, for the most part, the fly will always retain some profile to it. It will always look buggy under water.

The last reason reverse-hackle flies are popular with tenkara is the ability to impart motion into the fly. This is a unique trait of the sakasa kebari and something I believe gives them an edge. The reverse hackle will open and close depending on how the fly is manipulated. As you pull on the fly, it will open wide, and as the line relaxes, it gives the fly a chance to close slightly. This pulsing motion can very effective at luring fish.

One Fly

The first time I met Dr. Hisao Ishigaki, in May of 2009, he was visiting the US to give a talk about tenkara at the Catskills Fly Fishing Center and Museum in New York.

He started the event by giving a fly-tying demonstration. In approximately 50 seconds he tied a fly using black sewing thread, literally bought at a dollar store, and some cheap brown hackle he had brought. I didn't know what bug he was trying to imitate, but it seemed like it could pass off as just about any bug I could think of. And it was simple and quick to tie.

The Catskills area in New York, I should note, is considered one of the cradles of modern fly-fishing and fly-tying in the United States. So, when he tied that fly in 50 seconds with only two materials, most people watching him probably expected that to be the first of several patterns he would tie. After he tied the same fly a couple of more times someone asked what was next. Dr. Ishigaki responded, "This is it. This is the only fly I have used for the last 10 years."

There was a gasp by the audience, but Dr. Ishigaki went on to explain that most experienced tenkara anglers don't change flies. Tenkara anglers, he said, focus on technique and presentation instead of the fly pattern. Each tenkara angler has their "one fly," yet all their flies are different from one another. Since each angler thinks his fly is better than another's, but they all catch fish, we can take it to mean that just about "any fly" is okay.

Artificial flies are designed to represent bugs and thus fool fish into thinking they are food. Tenkara flies however, do not imitate a particular bug at a particular point in its life cycle. Rather, tenkara flies are more suggestive in nature. They suggest just about any bug that is in the water. This suggestive rather than imitative approach leads to incredible versatility, which in turn allows for simplicity. If one fly can suggest a large variety of bugs found in the water, then there is no need to carry so many fly patterns with us.

Rather than following the "match-the-hatch" dogma of western fly-fishing, which necessitates studying life cycles of bugs, tying a plethora of fly-patterns, second-guessing your every fly choice, consulting hatch guides, stopping by stores to see what fly is hot, and carrying around multiple fly boxes with dozens of patterns in each and in multiple colors, trust the one fly and learn how to use it.

Dr. Hisao Ishigaki ties the "Ishigaki kebari"
at the first tenkara demonstration in the U.S.

Besides the benefit of not carrying as many boxes of flies, there are other benefits to this approach. First, your fly spends more time in the water. If we were to change flies 20 times over the course of a day, and every time it took 3 minutes, that's an entire hour of fishing time just wasted by changing flies.

Second, what is to say the next pool was not going to produce a fish with the first fly we had on? The game of second-guessing our fly choice every time a fish doesn't take it can be very tiring and is a confidence killer. This is by far the most difficult concept of tenkara to embrace; yet it is also the most liberating. It is the part of tenkara that will allow you to simplify your fly-fishing more than anything else.

My Journey to Using One Fly

I was as skeptical as anyone when Dr. Ishigaki introduced me to the idea of using one fly regardless of the situation. For my first year or so of tenkara fishing I continued following the "match-the-hatch" approach and just occasionally fishing with the tenkara fly Dr. Ishigaki introduced me to.

But the idea of relying on one fly that could look like anything in the water rather than carrying boxes of flies in an attempt to imitate every bug greatly appealed to me.

In 2010, almost exactly a year after I first met Dr. Ishigaki and learned that a whole group of people didn't change flies when fishing, I visited him at the Itoshiro River in the Gifu Prefecture of Japan. This was my first trip to Japan exclusively to fish.

The rivers we fished were not unlike many of the waters I was used to fishing in California, although the forests were much lusher. They reminded me more of the streams in the Pacific Northwest and in the Appalachians, where deciduous trees take the place of pine forests.

We fished together for four entire days from morning to sunset. I learned the term *asamazume*, which indicated the period of high bug and fish activity early in the morning. And also *yumazume*, which described the period of higher fish activity in the evening. The fish didn't bite quite as much in the middle of the day, though we fished through the day and stopped only for a lunch break. The bug hatches were sometimes prolific. I saw large size-8 mayflies flying around every day, small caddis flies, some stoneflies, not to mention the numerous damselflies and midges.

Sometimes I'd point out the big mayflies fluttering around to Dr. Ishigaki. He'd look at them and shrug. Then, one perfect mayfly landed in his vest. In the US this would have immediately prompted anglers to find the closest-sized Adams flies in their box. I pointed the mayfly out to Dr. Ishigaki, and again he shrugged, this time as if to say, "Okay, nice, now let's keep fishing."

The mayfly that landed on Dr. Ishigaki's vest.

I decided this trip was my chance to learn how to use one fly and work on my technique. Ahead of the trip I had tied up a bunch of flies that looked like Dr. Ishigaki's, using just black sewing thread and cheap hackle. Unfortunately I didn't tie enough of them.

On our fourth day of fishing together, I caught a branch and lost my last Ishigaki kebari. Rather than asking him for flies, I decided to use what I had in my box. I pulled my closest match, a red-bodied fly with softer hackle and asked him, "Is this fly okay? " He said, "Oh yes, beautiful fly, okay, of course."

That fly didn't last long; the tight area we were fishing was consuming my flies. I tied on a slightly smaller fly and asked him if that was okay. He nodded, and I proceeded to lose it moments later.

Trying to at least continue using a reverse-hackle style fly, I pulled the last reverse-hackle fly out of my box. It was bright yellow and larger than the ones I had been using, perhaps a size 10. "Is this fly okay?" I asked him somewhat embarrassed about not being well prepared. He laughed out loud and with a big smile responded, "Yes, any fly okay!"

By the end of this trip to Japan, the bugs were interesting to look at in the same way birds are, but they were no longer as relevant to my fishing. "Any fly is okay" became my mantra.

Since 2011 I have carried essentially one fly pattern. With that one pattern, which I carry in four variations (three sizes, and two colors of the middle size), I have fished tumbling mountain streams, slow spring creeks, and the occasional lake with some of the most experienced fly anglers anywhere. I have fished from West to East coast in the US, and also in Argentina, Brazil, Italy, Japan, and in the UK. On all those trips I carried the same flies with me and caught at least as many trout as the person next to me who was matching the hatch.

It was not easy to give up my dozens of fly patterns, and then the "just-in-case" flies that had stayed in the corner of my fly box for a while after that trip. But with many days of fishing, learning the techniques to lure trout, and catching them without changing flies, I eventually built the confidence to leave the other flies behind.

I won't say it is a foolproof way to fish, or that it will be the most effective way to fish 100 percent of the time. But if it gets me to continue catching fish while not having to carry a bunch of stuff and continually second-guess my fly options, then I'm happy.

In 2011, I gave a clinic at Rocky Mountain National Park about the idea of not changing flies. One of the attendees was Mark Cole, an experienced fly angler and fly-fishing instructor. He was taking notes that day. A couple of years later he told me that on that day I had said, "The one fly approach works very well—until it doesn't." So far it has worked just fine.

Tenkara Fly Patterns
Beyond the simple reverse hackle flies found in the fly boxes of most tenkara anglers, it must be noted there is also great variety to be found in tenkara flies.

Since 1975 Mr. Yoshikazu Fujioka has been researching the historical and regional tenkara flies from around Japan. In 2010, after much communication with him via emails, I finally had a chance to fish with him in person.

When I met him, Mr. Fujioka presented me with a fly box containing the re-creation of about 20 of the fly patterns from different regions of Japan. Not all had the typical reverse hackle. Some were a bit more elaborate than others; one used the hair of the flowering ferns (*zenmai*) as dubbing. Some had stiffer hackle, etc.

The following year, Mr. Fujioka created a chart grouping the tenkara flies he had gathered over the years. Although the most popular and characteristic tenkara flies have the reverse hackle, you will notice that not all of them do.

Visit Mr. Fujioka's website at **www.hi-ho.ne.jp/amago**

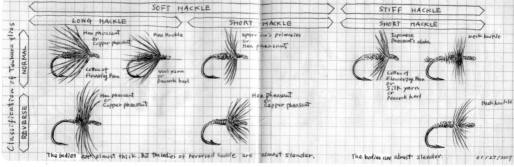

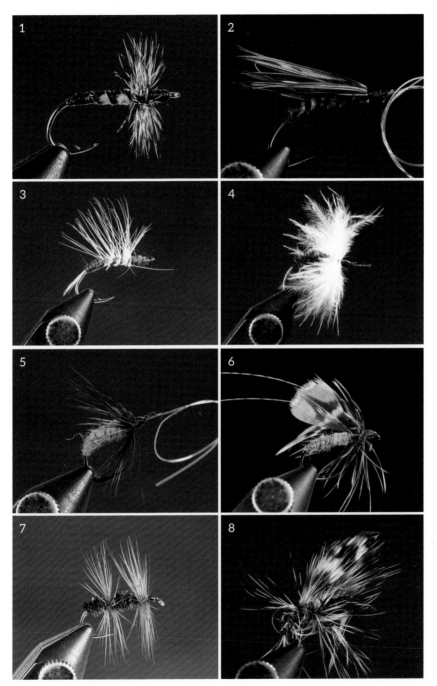

1. *Mamushi kebari,* tied using a strip of snake skin "mamushi", tied by Mr. Hirata
2. *Arakawa kebari,* tied by Mr. Yoshikazu Fujioka 3. *Awa-Nakagawa kebari,* tied by Mr. Yoshikazu Fujioka 4. *Itoshiro kebari,* tied by Mr. Yoshikazu Fujioka 5. *Koromori kebari,* tied by Mr. Yoshikazu Fujioka 6. *Nikko kebari,* tied by Mr. Yoshikazu Fujioka 7. *Shokawa kebari,* tied by Mr. Yoshikazu Fujioka 8. *Shotaro kebari,* tied by Mr. Ishimaru Shotaro

How to Tie Tenkara Flies

All fly anglers will agree there is something special about catching fish with a fly you tied yourself. You can start tying flies right now with only four things: a hook, sewing thread, a feather and scissors. And, in only 6 basic steps:

AMANO TYING

10kara.co/14

1- Secure the thread onto the hook by a few wraps
2- Tie a feather on top of the hook
3- Wrap that feather around the hook about 3 or 4 times
4- Secure the end of the feather
5- Wrap more thread on the shank of the hook
6- Tie the thread off with a knot.

Mr. Katsutoshi Amano ties his flies without the use of a vise. He started tying flies without one and by the time someone gave him a vise to hold the hooks he was already used to tying them by hand, quickly and efficiently.

Mamushi Kebari

Simple and dangerous don't cross paths all that often. Fly tiers are renowned for visiting thread and yarn shops more often than braving dangers to find naturally occurring fly-tying materials. At the center of the simple, dangerous, and fly-tying Venn diagram you'll find the *mamushi kebari* being tied by Mr. Hisanobu Hirata.

In 2010, on my second visit to Japan, I was on my way to fish in Itoshiro with Dr. Ishigaki when we took a brief detour to a tackle shop in the town of Gujo, Gifu Prefecture. Like many tackle shops found in villages throughout Japan, this was a small shop next to a large river. It had a fairly small selection of items curated for the local angler's needs. It offered a little bit for tenkara, a little bit for bait fishing, and some gear for ayu fishing. But, unlike any other tackle shop found in Japan, this one was owned by Mr. Hirata, who had made his name tying the *mamushi kebari*, or snakeskin fly.

Snake skin, Hirata-san says, reflects light in just such a way that it is highly attractive to trout. So attractive, in fact, that for him it may be worth risking his life. He searches for the mamushi, a highly poisonous snake prolific in certain areas, kills them, and uses strips off their segmented bodies to tie flies. He will tie the strip of snakeskin near the bend of the hook, wrap it around the hook shank going forward, and tie it off. Then he will wrap hackle, typically short and stiff rooster hackle, near the eye of the fly.

If you will be tying a lot of flies it is probably worth investing in some tools. You can easily get a complete kit that will make fly-tying much easier than doing it by hand.

Get a simple fly tying kit and start tying your own flies

10kara.co/15

FLY TYING KIT

Shotaro Kebari

It is said that most flies are designed and tied to catch anglers rather than fish. Fish, after all, just want something that looks like food.

For most of my fly-fishing life, I expected the look of a fly to improve in relation to the time an angler has spent tying flies. Mr. Shotaro has been tenkara fishing and fly-tying since the late 1930s. Yet his flies were, for lack of a better term, the sloppiest I have ever seen.

What first struck me as a sloppy tenkara fly has turned out to be a representation of the pragmatic simplicity of the original tenkara angler. Touching thread turns, "perfect" proportions, and symmetry don't make for flies that work. When I posted a picture of Mr. Shotaro's fly on social media, the people responding to it seemed to appreciate knowing their flies didn't have to look pretty. "Experienced tiers tie flies that fish think are food...Buggy look is good!" said one. Another replied, "Maybe there is genius in the slop?"

The more I look at Mr. Shotaro's tenkara flies, the more they strike me as the work of an abstract artist with modern impressionist, or perhaps expressionist, tendencies. Bugs are not pretty, especially if they have tumbled in the currents and taken a beating. Perhaps one day their "sloppiness" will be more deeply appreciated, like a work of art. For now, know that your flies don't need to look pretty to catch fish.

The Ishigaki Kebari

The Ishigaki kebari has been the fly used by Dr. Ishigaki for nearly 20 years. It's very effective and possibly the simplest of flies.

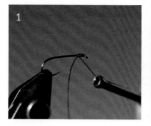

Place hook securely on vise, with hook shank parallel to your table. Secure thread onto the hook by wrapping thread over loose end of thread.

Trim excess thread. Wrap thread to the point where you want your hackle to begin (about 6-8 turns),

Secure the stem of rooster hackle (longer feather) with the tip facing toward eye of hook, and stem pointed to hook bend.

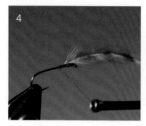

Wrap thread toward the end of the hook until where you want the hackle to stop (about 4-6 turns).

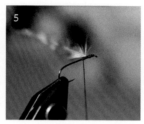

Wrap hackle around the hook, trying to have each turn be done behind the other toward hook bend. Stop where it meets thread.

You can make a fly more sparse, or bushier by doing fewer or more wraps. I typically do about 4 wraps of the hackle around hook.

Secure feather with 3 or 4 wraps of thread. Cut remaining feather.

Brush hackle forward to get fibers out of the way. You can build a collar with thread to get a more pronounced reverse hackle.

Your hook, feather and thread have started looking like a fly now.

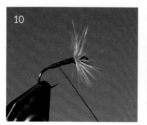

From here you will build the body of your fly with thread. Build it as thin or as thick as you wish.

Finish your fly with some type of knot. The objective is to trap your thread by wrapping thread around it and pulling tight.

10kara.co/16

TYING THE ISHIGAKI

The Takayama Kebari

The Takayama kebari is named after the region it's thought to come from. The peacock herl collar is the main characteristic of the so-called Takayama kebari.

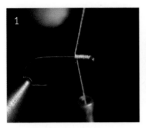

With the hook secured to the vise and parallel to your tying surface, secure the thread onto the hook so that the end is trapped.

With the soft-hackle "spade" type of feather, you will secure the feather by the tip. Remove the very soft fuzz at the thick end of the stem by ripping it back toward stem end.

Hold tip and brush all other fibers back to open feather. Secure the tip where you want the hackle to start. Try having the concave side of the feather facing up.

Start turning the hackle around the hook shank, toward the bend. Try to make the concave side face forward for the "sakasa" style fly.

Wrap the hackle back, securing the stem with 3 or 4 wraps of thread. Build a collar with thread for a more pronounced reverse hackle.

Cut off excess stem.

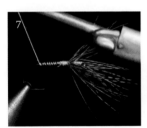

Start building the body of the fly with thread.

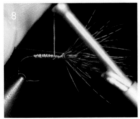

You can build the body as thin or thick as you want.

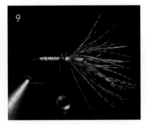

For variety, use the peacock herl strands to build a collar which also helps prevent feather fibers from sticking to the hook when wet.

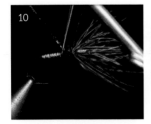

Peacock herl is a fragile material. You may want to twist two strands together, or twist the peacock herl around the thread for extra strength.

At this point you'll finish your fly by using a whip-finish knot, or half-hitches. Tip: a drop of super glue on the body of the fly will make it last much longer.

10kara.co/17

TYING THE TAKAYAMA

Thatched Roofs and Fly Tying with Masami Sakakibara

In 2013 I was back in Japan on my annual pilgrimage. It was my fifth visit to Japan and the third I'd spent learning from Mr. Masami Sakakibara, a.k.a. *tenkara no oni*, or "the tenkara demon."

My friend Go Ishii picked me up at a highway intersection close to where Dr. Ishigaki and I had been fishing in Nagano. From there we drove to the scenic Shogawa [river] valley, where the Shirakawa-go village of traditional thatched-roof houses is located. This was one of Mr. Sakakibara's favorite areas to fish and I could see why.

We spent the day catching amago and iwana, the native trout of the area. As evening fell upon us we retreated into the village. The old houses, built at a time when the villagers in the area were developing tenkara, transported us back to a simpler period.

The roofs of the *gassho-zukuri* houses were built steeply with dried straw and were over a foot thick. *Gassho* is the word used to describe when our hands come together in prayer like the steep roof angles that ensured the houses would withstand the weight of heavy snow that falls in the area.

This was not the kind of dwelling the original tenkara anglers would have lived in; theirs would likely have been less grand. The house had traditional features like *tatami* rooms and the *irori*, or sunken hearth used to heat up the house and to cook. While it had been retrofitted with modern amenities such as electricity, the low-wattage light bulbs, the dark wooden walls and the rice-paper sliding screens made it feel like it must have felt two hundred years ago. Smoke exhaled by the group's cigarettes filled the air and gave the interior a dreamlike feel.

After dinner Mr. Sakakibara brought out the fly-tying vise his father, a metal worker, had made for him decades earlier. Its patina revealed the decades of handling by Sakakibara-san and was the only vise he used.

We spent the evening enjoying good wine and watching Mr. Sakakibara tie the large flies he would use to catch more amago and iwana the next day.

Zenmai Kebari

Spring can bring to mind the beginning of fishing season or brutal snowmelt runoff, depending on where you live. For some people in Japan, it brings to mind foraging for *zenmai*, a mountain vegetable also known as a fiddlehead fern or flowering fern (*Osmunda sp.*).

Zenmai can be found in many parts of the world, most notably throughout Japan and in several of the wetter parts of North America. In early spring, the prime time for picking the fiddleheads for food, a fuzzy material covers the young fiddleheads. The fuzzy material forms a thick cover over the zenmai. Those who forage for zenmai for food wish it wasn't there, as the removal of the fuzz is a laborious part of preparing the zenmai for eating.

Historically, the material was used to make thread and clothing. It's said to have relatively waterproof properties. And, at one point in time, a fisherman, who must have been cursing the task of cleaning the fuzz off the zenmai, decided that perhaps it would make good fly-tying material as dubbing. And so the zenmai kebari was created. While its waterproof quality should make it a buoyant fly, the most interesting property I have noticed is that a bubble of air tends to form within its fibers. Some western fly anglers swear by the reflective quality of bubbles of air trapped in their sinking nymphs, and so they attempt to create that effect by using desiccants. Zenmai is a natural material that accomplishes the same thing in a simpler manner.

Tenkara Nets

One other item commonly found in the hands of tenkara anglers is the tenkara net. Tenkara nets, also known as *tamo*, look exquisite but are also highly functional. Their highly functional design along with their organic beauty is what drew me to learn more about tenkara nets.

It is not known whether the early tenkara fisherman deliberately designed the nets to look the way they do, or if it was simply a matter of working with what nature gave them. But, tenkara nets feature a highly functional design.

You will notice there is an angle between the handle and the frame of the net. This allows the net to be used comfortably throughout different stages of fishing; when not in use the net can be slipped into one's belt with only a small point of contact touching the angler's back, the handle and frame stay comfortably away from the back and within easy reach.

Further, when the angler scoops a fish into the net, the net can be placed between the knees, pressed behind the knees or even slipped on the side of one's wading belt to free up the hands in order to handle the fish.

TAMO MAKING

10kara.co/18

Tenkara nets are traditionally made from one single tree branch. They are crafted through a unique artisanal process where the maker first must find the perfect branch and then work with it to create the finished product. Just as no two branches on a tree look the same, no two nets are alike.

It's beyond the scope of this book to go into detail about net making, so this will just serve as an introduction.

Yukihiro Yoshimura

Mr. Yoshimura was the heir to the 250-year-old Mankyu tackle-shop, a fifth-generation store in Gifu city in Japan. In the late 1970s his father showed him the nets used for tenkara and taught him how to make them. The younger Yoshimura-san was impressed by the woodcraft and started making tenkara nets himself. He became the master of a disappearing craft.

In 2011, while spending two months in Japan, I connected with Yoshimura-san for a visit. I showed up at the Mankyu shop with my friend Kazuhiro Kuwata, who served as a translator. The shop looked more like an office than a store. There was a table with stacks of papers. Some cardboard boxes and a few nets spread around the office, but not displayed in any particular way.

I had been trying my hand at making tenkara nets for about a year or so and had made several nets. But it was a learning process. Out of my first 10 or so nets, I was proudest of two. I brought those two along to show Mr. Yoshimura what I had been attempting to do. He didn't bring up any criticism of the nets, but I suspect that was more of an effort to encourage my interest in the craft.

Toward the end of my visit Mr. Yoshimura invited me to come back and spend a day with him at the workshop. With over 45 years of experience making tenkara nets, he had a lot to share.

I returned a week later to spend the day with him. This was the first time he ever allowed someone to watch him and document the process. The Mankyu workshop was a huge warehouse filled to the roof with branches that had been drying for years waiting for their turn in the master's hands. He showed me the perfect branches that had been collected all over Japan, some of which featured deep scars created by deer chewing on the wood. These details, "flaws" if you will, were highly desired and made the nets unique. He steamed portions of nets to be bent. Finally he taught me how to connect the side branches into a net and how to finish it.

I planned to return the following year to record the process in more detail. Sadly, Mr. Yoshimura passed away the year after I visited. I am honored to have learned his craft and to be able to share it.

—
part
three
—

learning tenkara

Learning Tenkara

Tenkara is simple to understand and easy to learn, but as with anything simple on the surface it also provides opportunities for lifelong learning and mastery. As you delve deeper into tenkara, the pages that follow will help you become a proficient angler who will rely more on your technique and experience than on the tackle in your kit.

Reading Water

Reading water to identify locations fish are likely to be is not complicated when we learn two basic things about fish: Fish are looking for food, and they don't want to spend much energy searching for it. Currents bring along food, while calm water gives fish a place to hang out and rest. Generally speaking, we can find most fish where food is brought to them and they don't have to be fighting currents (spending calories gained from the food they eat). The most likely places are seams—the places where fast and calm water meet.

Some seams will be very easy to identify by looking at the surface. In many mountain streams, boulders will break the currents and form calm pockets behind them while the currents coming in on the sides of the boulder will bring food. These pockets of calm water near heavy currents are easy to distinguish and good places to cast a fly.

Calm water can also often be found along the banks of rivers and streams. Tip: Never ignore the bank closest to you, often we will walk right up to the bank, while paying attention to the other side of a stream, even when the water nearest us is very promising and casting from a few feet away to the closest bank would produce fish. The fish are not always on the other side!

Additionally, there are many other features we can use to quickly identify where the fish are. Logs will often have fish underneath them or around them. Foam lines indicate where currents have met calm water and where food may be coming from, "foam is home" goes the adage. Weed beds offer comfortable places for fish to spend time as they break currents and protect them from predators while at the same time hosting insect life and crustaceans for fish to prey on.

There are also slightly less obvious spots to look for and which are typically ignored by most anglers, either because they are harder to identify or too difficult to fish with their equipment (but easily fished with tenkara).

Surface currents can be different from those deeper below since there may be submerged rocks that will slow the currents down, or channel them into faster speeds.

In relatively featureless waters, look for very subtle "soft" water, often formed as a slick that is very slightly calmer than the water around it. These slicks can be an indication of breaks in the current beneath the surface, and thus good places for fish to hang even if deeper in the water.

Sandy bottoms near rocky areas show you where the water is calm below the surface since sand is easily disturbed by currents and doesn't gather in fast water. When I find sandy areas I like to keep an eye on them for a couple of minutes. I find that fish often will hold in above the rocks near sand, perhaps to remain camouflaged, but will come in and out of the sandy area. The contrast between a fish (usually dark) and the lighter sand beneath may make it easier to spot them.

Lastly, do not ignore **micro-pockets** when fishing mountain streams. In tumbling streams fast water may be broken into tiny pockets, from 10 to 30 inches in diameter. With a rod and reel setup, or with lures or bait, it is very difficult if not impossible to fish these, so most people ignore them. Yet these pockets hold fish. Tenkara is the ideal setup to place a fly in these areas without the fast water around them dragging our line and fly out of them before a fish can see it.

Cast into these areas and try to get your fly to spend a couple of seconds there. I'll walk you through some examples of waters and features where it is worth casting your fly.

Stream Anatomy

PLUNGE

RUN

WHIRL
POOL

MICRO
POCKET

FOAM LINE

HEAD

POCKET

MIDDLE

TAIL

Where to Find Fish and Cast Your Fly

READING WATER

10kara.co/19

Types of Waters

Fast Streams and Pocket Waters

In a tumbling mountain stream you will often see well-defined pockets. This is usually referred to as pocket water.

The location where fish are likely to hold is generally easy to identify. Try casting in the calmest waters you find. Fish will hold where currents are bringing them food but they don't need to fight currents. Don't spend too much time where the water is very shallow, especially when there are good pools that may be holding fish.

There are usually a lot of very small pockets that anglers ignore. Even pools that are barely two feet in diameter can hold fish, and it is always worth casting the fly to them. Cast on the upstream of foam lines, behind and in front of rocks, and places where water forms whirlpools.
To fish pocket waters try to get the fly to hang for as long as possible in the calmest waters.

Ben Furimsky lands a nice brown
on the Gunnison River in Colorado.

Larger Rivers

Sometimes people think tenkara is not adequate for fishing in larger rivers. Wider rivers are some of my favorite waters to fish. Keep in mind that any river is a collection of small streams. The fish rising on the other side of a larger river are just trying to distract you and there are lots of fish within reach. Rivers will have the same features as mountain streams and slower rivers, albeit some of these features may be harder to notice as they are found beneath the surface. Finding slower slicks next to heavier currents, targeting any features you see, or simply letting the fly hang in the water as long as you can are good tactics.

One way to approach the intimidating aspect of fishing a large river with a tenkara rod is to look at it as a series of smaller streams side-by-side. This can allow anglers to focus more on the waters they can effectively fish. Rather than trying to overreach in a cast, drop your line where it will go and fish it as you would any smaller river.

Walking along the bank of a large river and casting directly upstream along the bank is also a good way to fish.

Dr. Hisao Ishigaki
fishes the Firehole River, MT.

Slow-moving Water

In slower-moving meandering streams you may find the occasional obvious
spot, but there are many other places that will hold fish too. Slower-moving
streams offer fish a lot more places to hold without spending a tremendous
amount of energy. However, these present the challenge of requiring a careful
approach so you don't spook the fish.

Banks of slower-moving streams are great places to target. Often the currents
undercut them and create a protected spot for fish. A fish will hold there until a
juicy bug drifts by and tempts the fish to move out and take it.

Tree branches and roots hanging over banks might make getting a fly there
slightly more challenging, but it will be well worth the effort because these
areas often hold fish.

Unlike in faster streams, which force fish to seek slower waters, in slower-moving streams fish may take advantage of all the food being brought to
them by currents and will be found directly in the path of the current.

Fishing Lakes and Ponds

Much of this book is focused on mountain streams and rivers. That's where tenkara shines brightest. But a tenkara rod is also a good tool that can be used to fish in lakes and ponds with great effectiveness

My main experiences fishing tenkara in lakes comes from hiking to alpine lakes in scenic landscapes in search of trout, or fishing the slightly less scenic ponds close to home for panfish and bass (I've also been known to do some tenkara fishing from a stand-up paddleboard in lakes, and that can be a hoot!).

In a strict sense, from the eyes of the Japanese angler, tenkara done in a lake may cease to be tenkara and becomes fishing with a tenkara rod. It's a subtle distinction, and I think it's better not to get too caught up on that. Suffice it to say many people use tenkara rods in lakes.

People often focus on the limitation of not having a reel and running line when fishing with tenkara in lakes and ponds. Sure, you cannot cast to the other side of a lake, but that doesn't mean there aren't plenty of fish to be found nearby and within reach (25 to 40 feet away). I like to point out that the fish rising on the other side of a lake are just trying to distract you anyway.

My tactics in a lake usually consist of hiking around its shore slowly to see if I can find signs of fish or structures that may hide them such as a tree that fell into the lake. Also, inlets into lakes bring food to fish and are great places to fish. Sometimes I'll be a bit lazier and not move much, but rather wait for cruising fish to find me.

While I cover the main techniques for tenkara later in this book, I'll share here my favorite techniques to fish in lakes.

Letting the fly sink (I'll vary the depth that I aim to get the fly), and once the fly has sunk twitch the fly slightly a couple of times or doing a couple of pulls and let it sink again. The twitching and pulling lets fish know there is a fly around them and entices the fish to take it.

Lowering the fly only onto the surface of the water a few times as if it were a bug touching the water a few times, tempting a fish to come up and take it.

Skating the fly on the surface of the water. This can be a killer technique for beaver ponds with aggressive brook trout.

The author's wife, Margaret, fishes the foam in a stream in Rocky Mountain National Park

Features

"Foam is home"

In the image on the left, Margaret finds a prime fishing spot: a foam line above a large boulder. The water closest to her is darker than on the other side, indicating deeper water for the fish to hold. Foam is showing exactly where the food is coming to the fish. The fish are likely holding right in front of the large boulder, which deflects the water and forms a comfortable cushion of slower moving water underneath the surface. She fished it from upstream since the willows next to the boulder would make it hard to fish from downstream.

Submerged Boulders

Submerged boulders can be neglected in favor of more obvious holding places that break the water's surface. But, keep there are a lot of rocks beneath the surface that will be good holding spots for fish. If a fly is well presented to them, perhaps by pausing it in place in front of the submerged rock, we can get the fish to come up and take it.

Sometimes there are no obvious features in a river but there will be subsurface features. Polarized glasses can come in very handy in spotting those.

Riffles

Riffles are a shallower and more turbulent feature found in rivers, some mountain streams, and meandering creeks. They are often in between pools.

Although the location of a fish in a riffle may not be evident, it's always worth casting a fly there. Riffles may hold fish for longer periods of time if there are larger submerged rocks where trout can hang out.

Riffles can be seen as a transitioning feature with many fish passing by on the way to another location. Riffles are a food-delivery system into pools, and one of my favorite places to fish is where a riffle spills into a pool.

Stealthy as a *Neko*

Once I was fishing in Nagano prefecture with Ishigaki-sensei and our friend
Kazumitsu Suzuki. We arrived at a stream with crystal clear water and I immediately saw the small Iwana darting away.

Just as well as we could see them, they could see us.

"*Neko,*" said Suzuki-san. I turned around to see him imitating a cat's crawl with
his hands. "Like cat" he said. Cats tend to approach so slowly that they go
unnoticed by the unsuspecting prey; the Japanese word for cat is *neko*.

EXAMPLE OF FISHY WATER

In this image fly-fishing author Ed Engle targets the very good-looking pool on the other side of the stream as John Gierach scouts for more waters upstream.

EXAMPLE OF FISHY WATER
Masako Tani fishes a seemingly featureless river by keeping the fly in the water for long drifts over submerged rocks and paying attention to subtle surface currents.

EXAMPLE OF FISHY WATER

Margaret fishes the very small pockets and runs that are often ignored by other anglers. Each of them has great potential to hold fish interested in eating a fly.

EXAMPLE OF FISHY WATER

Tim Gasperak works several spots in a prime pool that features foam lines, deep water and currents that bring food and his fly to the fish.

Approaching and Covering Water

In order to improve your chances of catching more fish, it is important to approach water stealthily and cover it well.

When possible, start casting before you reach the shore of the stream or river. Stream banks offer great shelter to fish and are a favorite hangout for many hungry trout. Work the water methodically by breaking the run into smaller sections and looking for the best positions to fish each section.

If the stream is relatively open, cast to the closer bank first and work your way out, hitting as many seams or features as you can until you get your fly to the other side of the stream. Remember, the fish are not just on the other side of a stream.

While every stream will be different and you have to be very flexible and adapt to the environment around you, in an ideal scenario this is how I typically cover most pools.

Positioning and Moving

Positioning is very important in fishing. And, fishing with a fixed length of line, as we do with tenkara, can teach us a lot about fishing as it often forces us to position ourselves in the ideal location for the best presentation of our flies. I often like to compare fishing with tenkara to taking photographs with a camera without a zoom. When your camera has no zoom, you will need to move a foot forward or backward, or a bit to the left or to the right, to take the best possible picture of your subject. It just so happens that my favorite photographs are the ones I take with a fixed-lens system (in fact, most images in this book). When I walk a foot closer to my subject, I achieve a much better composition than when I lazily zoom in from a distance.

Sometimes moving just one or two feet up or downstream or forward into the stream will allow you to achieve the best possible presentation for a particular spot. It is tempting to try fishing every spot from one fixed location, but I highly encourage moving slowly every couple of casts. When you feel your line is getting picked up and dragged by the edge of a current, try moving slightly toward it. Or move upstream a couple of feet when you feel you have to extend your arm to reach your upstream target pocket of water. Get in a routine of moving a step or two after every 2 to 3 casts in a large pool or every 4 to 5 casts in a larger river.

It is important that your movement be slow. Small steps help with that. Fish are sensitive to movement more than anything else, particularly fast movement. This is especially important in very clear or calm water. Water that is murky or turbulent can hide your movement and you can get away with moving a bit faster.

Try watching a crane in a pond, and you'll see how slowly it approaches its target. It will take a few seconds to lift a leg, move it forward in slow motion, and then take another few seconds to place its leg down.

My friend Eiji Yamakawa talks about following the "10-centimeter rule" when you are ready to move. Yamakawa-san says, "From my experiences, fish cannot notice that somebody is approaching them if you approach them at a speed of 10 cm per second or slower." He suggests moving 10 cm (4 inches) per second as a rule of thumb. Following this rule would mean that when you want to move about a foot it should take about 3 seconds to do that, or approximately 10 seconds to move 3 feet.

Positioning is also important when landing fish. Moving a couple of feet downstream toward the fish can allow you to bring the fish to a calmer pool of water while also not fighting the current quite as hard. You do not have to run with a fish, just position yourself better to successfully bring the fish in. Walk and guide the fish to calmer water. Don't be afraid to move a bit. With time you'll develop a knack for where to position yourself to best land a fish. Just be sure not to move too fast or toward places you may want to fish next, lest you scare fish away.

Upstream or Downstream?
While you can fish moving up or downstream, I generally prefer to move upstream as I fish. However, even when I am generally moving upstream I may also fish particular section of water facing downstream to change my presentation or get to fish that may be hard to reach otherwise.

There are a few points in favor of fishing upstream. First, if you hook a fish on the tail end of the pool (downstream end) it is easier to bring the fish toward you downstream, assisted by the current. After hooking fish at the tail end of a pool you can fish the middle part of the pool and then the head of the pool where the fish have not been spooked.

Anglers often talk about fishing upstream because that's the direction fish are often facing and they are not likely to see you. I do not think that's a good reason for fishing upstream. A fish's field of view is very wide, and as it sways with the currents its field of view is nearly 360 degrees around it. Thus, a fish is able to detect predators moving in from any direction. Whatever direction you move, just move slowly and try to keep a low profile or hide behind obstacles such as large boulders or brush to avoid detection.

A good point in favor of moving upstream is stream etiquette. If two anglers find themselves in the same stream with one moving up and the other downstream, eventually they will cross paths. When they do, the water upstream from the angler moving down and the water downstream from the angler moving up will be ruined for a while. If both are moving in the same direction, with a good amount of space in between them to rest the pools, they can fish all day long without getting on each other's way.

My favorite reason to move upstream is being able to see features in the water a bit better. While I can identify some good spots to cast a fly when I am moving downstream, I find that elevated rocks often hide the prime spots, whereas moving upstream often reveals all the best spots to fish.

Here's a view of the same stream and its features as seen from downstream (top), and from upstream (bottom).

Further, moving upstream offers good opportunities to hide from fish.

Chikara Yokota uses a boulder to hide while fishing for very spooky trout.

Dr. Ishigaki does the same hiding downstream.

Dondon, Dondon!
Move, move!

One of the first fishing terms I learned in Japanese was "*dondon, dondon*."

This was my first visit back to Japan since I had discovered tenkara. I was particularly interested in learning more about the presentation techniques Dr. Ishigaki had talked about the year before.

The waters we fished varied quite a bit; they went from very narrow to wide. They had a lot of coverage in some areas but were completely open in others. There were also steep tumbling areas and some that were more meandering and calmer. It was a great stream to learn different tactics.

The next day, as we continued to fish the Itoshiro River, one of the only catch-and-release rivers in Japan, Dr. Ishigaki would follow me and observe my technique. I tried to impress upon him that I was paying attention to the techniques he taught me. If the pool looked good, I'd try a couple of dead drifts, then pulsate the fly a few times, then pause or pause and drift, and perhaps even pull it across like a streamer.

"*Jozu*," (perfect) he'd sometimes say, complimenting my form. Though later I learned that sometimes "Jozu" is often said when there is room for improvement.

Other times he'd give me some tips to improve my technique with words like "*yukuri*" indicating I should slow the movement of a pulsing fly; or he'd point at a spot and say "*asoko*" (there).

In one particularly good-looking pool I tried a few different techniques to see if I could coax a fish. "*Dondon, dondon*," I heard him saying. Not knowing what that meant, I turned to see him prompting me to move with a wave of his hand. Three or four casts into the next pool, I'd again hear, "*Dondon, dondon*."

Dondon, I later learned, literally means "gradually," and it may be the most understated "technique" in our arsenal.

In Dr. Ishigaki's eyes I was a bit of a camper, someone who finds a pool and "camps" until hooking a fish. I never considered myself a camper. One of my favorite things about fishing streams, after all, is seeing what's around the next bend. But I admit the prospect of a fish can have a hypnotizing effect on me.

I have not completely become immune to the hypnotizing effect of watching a fish and wanting a particular fish to take my fly. But I have come to realize one of the most efficient ways to fish a stream is to move gradually from pool to pool, finding the fish that is willing to take our fly.

Typically I cast 3–4 times into a small pool from one direction and then move gradually on. If the pool looks big (say larger than 10 feet in diameter) or very fishy, then I may try 5 or 6 casts from one direction and move gradually to a different position to try a different presentation or just move on to the next pool. Sometimes just moving a couple of feet allows our fly to be presented just differently enough to entice a fish.

It is said that one must hear a foreign word an average of seven times to learn it. That day I must have heard "*dondon*" so many times that to this day I think *dondon* when I want to usher a student to move along.

Eiji Yamakawa gradually moves upstream searching for the next trout.

Letting Go vs. Persisting

When fishing pocket waters it is easy to know how far to move between spots near each other. Essentially we'll move from one small pocket or well-defined feature to another. But it can be hard to know when to move if we see fish.

When a fish shows interest in my fly but didn't come all the way to get it or turned away at the last second, then I will try it again a few times. I figure the fish is interested in eating but that perhaps that my presentation could be a bit better, and perhaps getting the fly to drift just a tad better can trigger the fish to take it.

If the fish came to grab my fly but I missed it and don't think he felt the hook (often when I didn't feel anything myself), then I will try again two or three more times. If he doesn't come back it is because he was spooked.

If I feel the fish, it is safe to assume the fish also felt the hook. In my experience, the fish will often become much more hesitant to strike again. I may try another couple of casts just because I am excited. On a rare occasion I may get a fish (usually a different one) to take my fly, but usually there is little hope and I'll just move on.

There is nothing wrong with staying a bit longer on a big pool and seeing what happens. In fact, in waters where the pools are large, deep, and more sporadic, staying in a place longer may be the way to go as there will be more fish holding and perhaps one of them will be willing to take a fly that goes past it.

One of the hardest things to do is determining it is time to move to a completely different location. If you have been fishing for quite some time without a bite, then it may be worth collapsing your rod, winding your line, and going for a hike.

We all have slow fishing days. Sometimes weather changes will put fish down in a whole region, other times the stream flow affects the fish's willingness to eat. And, yet other times you may be fishing an area where someone (or something) disturbed the habitat just before you got there.

If the water is running quite high, try going further upstream to find sections of the stream where not as much water has gathered into a high flow. If the water is running very cold, try going downstream into potentially warmer areas that receive more sunlight. If it's a very bright day, try heading into a section with more trees and shade. All these things can make a difference.

Dr. Ishigaki approaching a section
of the Itoshiro River, in Gifu Japan.

Casting

One does not have to go to summer camp or learn physics to learn how to fly cast, at least not with tenkara. Tenkara casting is very intuitive, and anyone can pick it up quickly. I often compare casting the tenkara line/fly with tossing a pebble at a target. Nobody has to teach you how to throw the pebble. You pick it up and your brain tells you what to do: lift the forearm up, then quickly move it down and release the pebble as your arm moves downward. The key is just to pick a target.

Your pebble may not always hit the tree the first time around. And there may be some tips others can share with you on how to get the pebble closer to your target. As long as you don't overthink it and focus on your target, then you already know 90% of what you need to know to cast your fly where you think the fish will be.

I will cover the foundations of a tenkara cast. These foundations will help you make good, effortless, precise casts.

Some general notes about fly-casting terms. In fly-casting, the backward motion—where you swing the rod tip up and toward the back to throw the line backward—is called the backcast. On the backcast you will have a very brief but well-defined stop at the vertical position. Then, you will quickly swing the forearm downward, stopping at roughly a 45-degree angle (2 o'clock position). This is called the forward cast.

While I will give you a good amount of in-depth and nuanced details about how to cast in this chapter, watching our casting video will take a couple of minutes and will give you most of what you need to know. It is definitely worth taking a couple of minutes to watch this video.

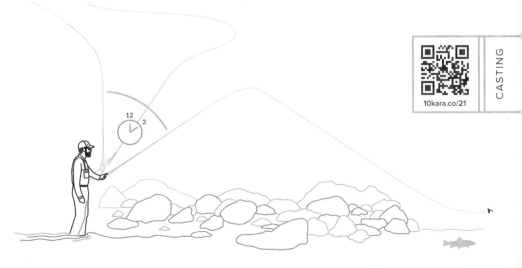

10kara.co/21

CASTING

Grip

The best and most common way to hold a tenkara rod while casting is with the index finger on top. First, this grip makes it so that you will point to where you want to cast, adding to its intuitiveness. Further, holding the rod with an index finger on top of the handle has the advantage of making your rod naturally stop at a vertical position (12 o'clock), which is exactly where it needs to stop on the backcast.

Try this little experiment: With your arm pointing up at approximately 45 degrees in front of you and a pointed index finger, try bending your wrist back and see where it stops. You'll notice it will be pointing skyward when it stops.

Now, compare that with having a thumb point forward and bending your wrist; your thumb will point back behind you, and your rod tip would be on the trees.

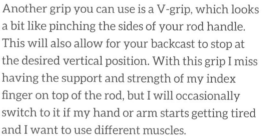

Another grip you can use is a V-grip, which looks a bit like pinching the sides of your rod handle. This will also allow for your backcast to stop at the desired vertical position. With this grip I miss having the support and strength of my index finger on top of the rod, but I will occasionally switch to it if my hand or arm starts getting tired and I want to use different muscles.

The grip should be relaxed. A tight grip on the handle, especially at the end of your forward cast, will mean your hand will not absorb the oscillation of the rod and the line will often be wavy as it approaches the water rather than stretch out in front of you.

One easy way to accomplish that is to place your thumb closer to the index finger (or even off the handle) and to support the rod handle with the part of your palm below the pinky finger rather than immediately below the index finger.

Hand Position

In tenkara there is no reel telling you where to hold your rod, so you can really hold the rod anywhere.

The best spot to hold the rod is right at the very end of the grip, with your hand supported by the butt end of the rod. This will give you a longer lever and make casting effortless. It is important to choose a rod with a rounded handle end to ensure comfortable gripping in this position.

As you move the hand up, the rod will feel lighter. While I normally hold the rod at the end, I will sometimes "rest" my hand higher up on the grip.

Finally, in tight spots with more trees overhead you can hold the rod well above the handle, on the blank of the rod, to instantly have a shorter rod.

Arm and Wrist

If you have ever been taught how to cast with a fly rod, you have likely been told, "Don't break your wrist!" Just know you were not doing it wrong, but rather just that you are naturally a tenkara angler! In fact, it is important that you use the arm and wrist together to cast well and effortlessly.

Everyone naturally bends their wrist back when learning how to fly cast. That is a natural motion for our arms to follow. Luckily, a good tenkara cast will use the wrist, too.

The basic cast will consist of bending the elbow to move the forearm up about 2–3 inches rapidly, and then allowing the wrist to bend naturally so that the index finger points up to the sky.

Moving the arm is what will give your rod the speed necessary to shoot the line back, while the natural wrist break will make the rod flex (load) and unflex to shoot the line out forward for you.

Using only the arm while keeping a stiff wrist makes the cast more laborious and will make it harder to cast longer lines.

At the same time, if you use only the wrist you may not generate enough speed and your wrist will start getting tired and possibly sore or even injured after a full day of casting.

Speed and Power

The backcast is the foundation of a good tenkara cast. It is the part of the cast that will make the rod load and work for you by propelling the line forward on your forward cast.

It is very important that the backcast be executed with speed. Often people want to move the rod back slowly and then try to throw the line by moving the arm forward fast and forcefully. This doesn't work very well. In fact, the opposite is usually the best: a fast backcast with a very quick but well-defined stop, and then a relatively slow forward cast (when casting against wind, the forward cast will also be fast).

If your cast is not going where you want it to, it is likely due to a backcast that is too slow or hesitant. I will cover some common casting problems later, but generally if the fly is not going far, put more speed and less hesitation on the backcast.

Now, there is a difference between speed and power. A frequent problem I see with people's casting is that they put too much power into their cast. This is particularly true with those coming from a western fly-fishing background where the lines are heavy. The tenkara cast requires minimal effort. My main advice is to cut your power in half, and then halve it again. Make the rod work for you. But, to make it work you need to move it quickly, albeit lightly, on your backcast.

Face the direction where you want to cast

While you can cast off your sides and in any direction you want, it's best to have your whole body facing the direction you want your fly to go. Often times I have seen an angler's cast improve dramatically just by rotating the body a couple of inches to directly face the target.

Line everything up

The best casts will come when every part involved in the cast is in a straight line. Get your upper arm, forearm, wrist, index finger, tenkara rod, and even your leg aligned.

Stance

Stance is not particularly important for casting with tenkara but in general I have found it best to have the foot on the side of the casting arm placed in front of my other foot and offset to the side slightly.

If you are a right-hand caster, have your right foot slightly forward. This helps achieve a longer reach. But having good balance is important for safety; sometimes it may be best to have the opposite foot forward for better balance.

Casting Variations

Sometimes we need to change our casting angles to avoid potential snags behind us, above us, or in front of us. Other times we will change our cast to get the fly into tricky spots. The basic tenkara cast can get us where we need the fly to go with very minor and intuitive changes in the angle and speed at which the rod will move.

It helps to think in three-dimensional terms when it comes to casting too. Sometimes it is necessary to not cast directly overhead, but rather slightly off to the side where the opening in the canopy is present.

Simply by stopping the rod at different positions, you can get your fly to stay away from trees behind you, shoot the fly under obstacles, and avoid branches directly above you.

I'd suggest ignoring instructions that make casting seem more complicated than this. Below are the variations you need to cast comfortably in just about any place.

Making a fly land under tree branches and overhung rocks: To shoot line under tree branches on the other side of a stream, you can stop your rod tip lower and closer to the water on your forward cast. This cast is also best done very quickly, particularly on the forward cast. You will move the rod between the 1:00 and 2:45 positions. With the rod tip stopping closer to the water, your line will travel lower and parallel to it, carrying the fly below the obstacle in front.

Stay away from trees above and behind: When there are a lot of branches overhead, you can simply shorten the casting stroke and stop your backcast before the rod gets to vertical position. This will ensure that not much line gets shot up and into tree branches.

This cast requires a much quicker stop on the backcast, making it fast and snappy. Since you will be using this in places with a lot more trees, it may also be useful to use a shorter line. If the stream is consistently tight, I recommend using a total line (line plus tippet) that is a foot or two shorter than the rod. Whenever possible look for openings where you can backcast your fly.

Side-arm Cast

When there are a lot of trees overhead and little in the way of openings, the side-arm cast can come in handy. This is essentially the same cast but moving the rod sideways, above the water, to get the fly upstream or downstream.

The motion will be very similar to the overhead cast, except it will be done to the side. By changing the angles where the rod tip stops it is possible to get the fly almost anywhere you want. Additionally, you can do a side-arm cast with very little motion by "water-loading" the rod tip. To do this let the line stretch downstream from you, which will make the rod tip flex and then use that to fling the fly back upstream.

The side-arm cast is also useful when casting against wind. By doing a side-arm cast with the rod tip/line low and close to the water you can take advantage of the area above a stream with less wind, right above the water.

Dapping

Dapping is the technique of lowering the fly or letting the wind carry it where you think the fish are. As it is probably clear by now, tenkara is not dapping, but dapping is one of the techniques we can use with a tenkara rod.

Dapping with tenkara is best done with a line that is either a bit shorter than the rod, or no more than 2 to 3 longer than the rod. Simply lower your fly to where you want to place it.

Slingshot Cast

This is the only cast that is not built on a variation of angles or speed of the rod, but rather based on the idea of using the rod to shoot the fly forward as if the rod were a slingshot.

In very tight situations you can pull on the line to flex the rod and let the rod slingshoot your line forward to your target. I have probably used this cast only a couple of dozen times in my 9 years of tenkara fishing. But, in the tightest of spots it was very helpful to know I could do it.

When executing the slingshot cast, you can hold the fly directly on the hook bend, or (my preference) hold the main tenkara line 3–4 feet above the fly.

Then, pointing the rod tip in the direction you want to cast, pull it until the rod is tensioned and then let go. Avoid holding the tippet too close to the fly, as you might get hooked when you let it go.

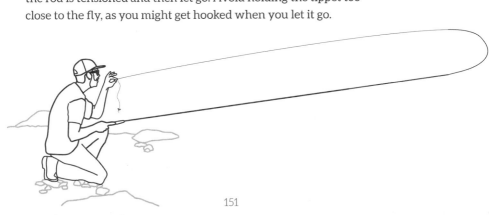

Good Form from Sakakibara Masami

While I, like anyone else, picked up basic casting with tenkara very quickly, it took me a while to acquire good form. But, later I realized that having good form makes things more effortless and more accurate regardless of the setup.

I was fortunate to spend an afternoon learning how to cast with long lines from Mr. Sakakibara Masami (aka. Tenkara no Oni). Mr. Masami is one of the most elegant casters I know. A lot of the tips I share come from his teachings.

The main thing I noticed was how little Sakakibara-san needed to move his arm and how effortless his casting was with a long line. I had attempted to use a long-line before, but it never looked elegant and certainly didn't feel effortless. His casts went right where he wanted, about 40 feet away, and the fly always landed first. He really made the rod work for him.

When I returned from that trip, I was determined to make my casts with long lines look as effortless and elegant as his. This was not necessarily because I wanted to use long lines, but because I knew that if I achieved accurate casting with long lines, it would help me improve my casting in general.

On my next few fishing trips I pulled out a long tenkara line. At first I just tried to get the line out there in any manner I could. Using a 13-foot rod and about 25 feet of line and 4 feet of tippet I was able to get half of my casts to land where I wanted them. Then I looked at my arm and remembered how little motion Sakakibara-san had put in his arm.

From then on I focused on making my arm and wrist look the way his did. The arm would move only a couple of inches and the wrist would move naturally. It was quick but effortless, with a minimal amount of power put into it. Just focusing on my arm and making it look the same as his dramatically improved my casting. I was getting more accurate and my casting more effortless. I did that for probably the next 30 casts or so. This allowed me to acquire the muscle memory of how my arm should be moving for effortless casting.

Sakakibara-san told me, "My brain does all the work for me." After I focused on acquiring good form for casting, I then focused on my target. And, just as he said, my brain did the rest for me, and casting became effortless and precise.

Look for Openings

The biggest frustration a novice tenkara angler will face is getting caught on trees behind or above. The solution for this is simple: Be aware of your surroundings.

The way to stay out of trees is to avoid them. Of course, that is usually easier said than done!

The reality is that we all get caught up. Luckily the frequency of losing flies goes down with experience and as we gain more awareness of our surroundings.

Always look up and behind you and identify where the best path for your rod to travel will be.

Any time you move a couple of feet, get to a new area or change body positions take a second to look above and behind you before casting. Very soon you will start doing this without a second thought.

Re-casting

Knowing when to pick up the line and cast it out again is a very important skill in tenkara.

One of the things you want in tenkara fishing is to have a tight line. The ability to keep the line tight is one of the main advantages of tenkara. A tight line allows the angler to detect strikes easily, set the hook properly, and to re-cast effortlessly. One way to ensure the line is tight is to pick it up and cast again at the right moment.

There is generally an area where we can notice the line remaining tight, where we can get an "effective drift." When casting directly upstream, for example, your fly starts drifting downstream toward you and you will start raising the tip of the rod to keep up with the drift.

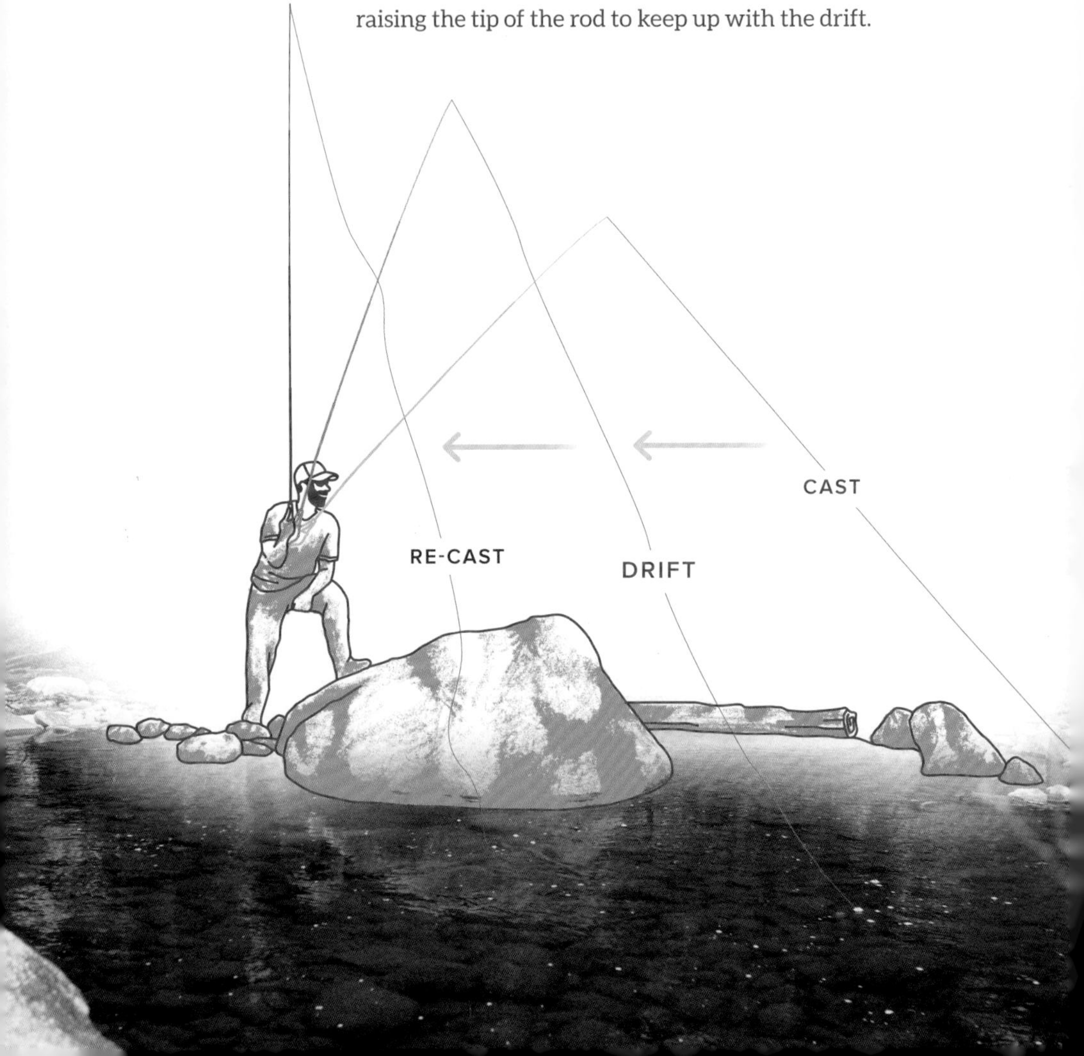

CAST

RE-CAST

DRIFT

With a line length about the same length as the rod, when the fly gets approximately below the tip of the rod the line will start getting slack, so it is important to pick up and cast again right before this happens. With a line longer than the rod, this will happen sooner (farther upstream).

When casting across a stream, the place where the line will be slack will vary depending on the currents you are fishing. Generally speaking, if the currents are bringing the fly slightly toward you, the line will get slack a bit sooner than when the current is drawing it away from you.

When the fly comes slightly toward you, you will want to recast when it gets close to being under the rod tip. When the current is pushing the fly away from you, you will be able to have much longer drifts by just continuing to follow the fly and then start lowering the tip of the rod.

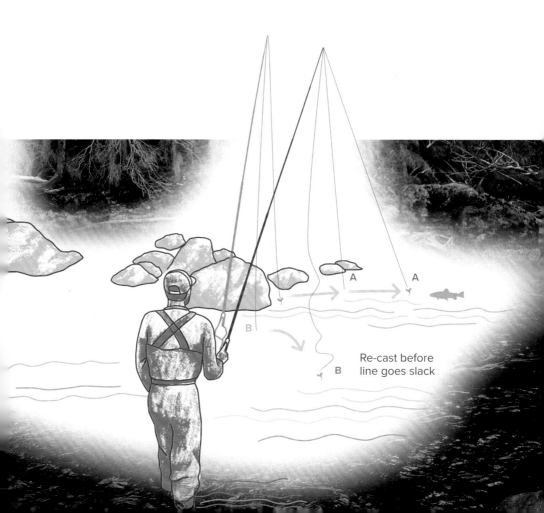

Re-cast before line goes slack

Make the Fly (or Fly and Tippet) Land First

The basic tenkara cast will present the fly to the fish without your main line touching the water. This allows for good drag-free presentations (where the line is not dragged by currents between you and the fish). But it is okay to have tippet landing on the water too, and sometimes it is a good thing to have the tippet also land on the water along with the fly.

If you are having trouble getting the fly to land first, try one of two things. First, you can stop the rod tip a bit higher on the forward cast. Also, relax your grip slightly as you stop the rod on the forward cast, this will keep the line from bouncing back.

Alternatively, almost as soon as the fly is about to land, and after you have stopped the rod, lift the rod tip just a couple of inches and stop the rod there.

When fishing upstream, aim at having only the fly land first with just about no tippet or line touching the water. This allows for a very natural presentation where the fly will come downstream with the current. If you are trying to sink the fly, then after presenting the fly first slowly lower the rod tip to start getting line in the water. Keep up with the sinking fly while maintaining a tight line.

When fishing across currents (either directly across the stream, slightly upstream, or slightly downstream), aim to have the fly and about a foot or two of your tippet land at approximately the same time.

The reason to do this is because if the fly is the only thing that lands first, then the weight of the line will pull the fly slightly toward you the moment it lands; this would make for an unnatural presentation in the critical first couple of seconds after the fly has landed. Having a couple of feet of tippet land with the fly helps anchor the fly to the targeted area and keeps the fly from dragging back.

When fishing downstream it can go either way. I generally prefer to land my fly first when fishing directly downstream, but I have found that when presenting the fly downstream, either fly first, or fly and tippet work fine. Typically if I want to dead-drift the fly, I will present the fly first, but I may try different techniques and a fly plus tippet may be desired.

Troubleshooting the Cast

I have noticed a few common problems that occur in casting. I hope this quick troubleshooting guide will help if you are having any problems with your cast.

My line doesn't straighten out in front of me/it wiggles at the end of the cast

Too much power. While you need speed in the cast, it is important not to use much force. Relax.

Too stiff a wrist, especially at the end of the forward cast. It is important to relax the wrist and hand at the end of the cast in order to absorb oscillation in the rod tip. Again, relax.

The line doesn't go out far/it piles up below the rod tip

Too slow a backcast, not throwing the line back, or not doing a backcast. Speed up the backcast, don't be afraid of throwing the line back (up).

Not having a well-defined stop on the backcast or forward cast. On the backcast stop the rod at 12 o'clock very briefly; on the forward-cast stop at around 2 o'clock and don't follow through.

Stopping for too long on the backcast. This will cause the line to fall to the back, and the rod will not shoot the line forward for you.

The fly doesn't land first/too much line landing on the water

Moving the rod too far back on the backcast (past the 12 o'clock position). If you are not doing it, try holding the rod with an index finger on top of the grip rather than thumb on top. And stop the rod sooner on the backcast.

Stopping the rod too low on the forward cast. Stop the rod tip a bit higher on the forward cast to shoot the fly down to your target.

Following through after the stop will cause the line to go down with the rod tip. Don't follow through.

Try pulling the rod back up a couple of inches right before the fly lands.

My fly is not going where I want it to/lack of accuracy on casting

Arm sticking out to the side rather than in a straight line in front of you. Body and face not facing the direction you want the fly to go.

It's just not working

You are likely overthinking it.
Pick a target, focus on it rather than on your cast, and just move your arm.

Casting in Wind

Wind is a fisherman's number-one enemy. It makes casting a fly challenging. However, there are ways to deal with wind.

Very fast forward cast: The main way to cast with tenkara consists of a relatively fast backcast followed by a somewhat slower and more relaxed forward cast. However, in the wind, you will still do a fast backcast, but you will follow that with a very fast and more powerful forward cast.

Low side-arm cast: Especially when fishing streams with any kind of gradient, there is a cushion of calm air right above the water. So, one way to cast against wind is to do a side-arm cast with the rod tip close to the water to take advantage of the calm-air cushion. You will also want to use a very fast and more powerful forward cast to overcome some of the wind.

Casting against strong winds can be done, but it can also be tiring and not much fun. While the techniques above are helpful, my main advice for very windy conditions is mainly to use the wind to your advantage. If you are fishing upstream and the wind is blowing against you, fish downstream. If the wind is stronger from one side of the stream, try wading across to use the wind to carry your fly for you, or walk a ways upstream to find places with less wind.

Long-lining

Many people see tenkara as "short-line fly-fishing." Yet, just as tenkara is not dapping and is not restricted to small streams, it needs not be restricted to the use of a short line. Using a long line, where the stream or river is more open, will open an entire new tenkara world for you.

My favorite rig for tenkara consists of a level line about 1 ½ times the length of my rod—approximately 20 feet of line on a 13-foot rod, plus 4 feet of tippet at the end of that. Occasionally, when fishing large bodies of water, I will use even longer lines—25 feet of line and 4 feet of tippet at the end of a 14-foot, 7-inch rod. This rig gives me about 40 feet of casting reach.

Casting with a long line is very accessible. It requires practice, for sure, but all the principles of casting apply to short lines and long lines alike. The main challenges you will face when you start experimenting with long lines in tenkara are keeping the line tight as you drift it in your favorite runs (it will be important to know when to re-cast) and landing fish.

For these reasons I recommend starting with a line the same length as the rod and gradually increasing the line length, about 3 feet at a time.

Short-lining

One rigging combination not discussed as much as it should be is the combination of a tenkara rod with a line shorter than the rod. This is one of the times when tenkara can resemble dapping (lowering the fly into the targeted spot).

We encourage people to start with a line that is the same length as the rod plus 4 feet of tippet and then try progressively longer lines. However, having a total line length about 1 or 2 feet shorter than the rod is a beautiful way to fish very tight streams with lots of cover.

While reach may be reduced, this combination gives great control over fly placement and it allows for a cast with an even shorter casting stroke where the line is not reaching trees above or behind the angler.

People are often surprised at how I can fish a very tight stream and not get caught on trees all around me. If I know I'm going to be fishing only a very tight stream, I will typically carry a shorter rod with me. However, occasionally I'll be prepared to fish a bigger portion of a stream and get into a section that is tight or a smaller tributary. In those cases I will usually pair my long rod with a very short line.

If I have a long level line, I will cut a few feet of line off the top end and re-tie the line to the rod tip (saving that line to rejoin later).

I also use this tactic when using adjustable rods. If I am fishing in a small stream with an adjustable rod, I will usually start with a line that is the same length as the shortest length of the rod. While fishing a tight stream, I may do something very counterintuitive, which is to make the rod longer! This in turn makes my line shorter than the rod and gives me greater control for fishing those tight areas.

Just don't go much shorter with your line than 2 feet shorter than the rod, as that will make it difficult to bring in the fish without resorting to collapsing a segment of the rod.

Kate Mason

Salome takes a little snag in stride.
Good attitude helps eliminate frustrations too.

Avoiding frustrations

Any sport comes with its own set of frustrations as you learn it. Fly-fishing is no different. Line will tangle on branches, flies will snag rocks and sometimes knots, which normally take us a couple of minutes to tie, will spontaneously appear perfectly tied in the two seconds you got distracted.

Despite its inherent simplicity tenkara is also not immune, but the good thing is that there are fewer elements to frustrate you and some easy things to learn that will help you avoid and occasionally deal with them.

There are three general principles that will assist anglers in reducing and dealing with potential frustrations, and thus increase the enjoyment of their fishing:

> **Be aware:** This is most important principle; being aware of the things that can snag your fly and working to avoid them will go a long way toward reducing the most common cause of frustrations to any angler: snags.

Whether you just arrived at the stream, just turned your body, or moved a few inches upstream, be aware of any branches hanging behind you, overhead, or in front of you. Take a second to look around and over your shoulders to identify where the line will travel when you cast and where it will land and avoid snags. I know, easier said than done, but this habit will quickly pay off.

> **Keep it simple:** Yes, that's the theme of this book, but it is worth mentioning here again.

When you have fewer elements in your rig (e.g. one fly rather than multiple) and carry fewer things with you, there will be fewer things to tangle up, to drop, and to forget. I have found that keeping my systems simple have greatly eliminated frustrations while I fish. Perhaps it is obvious, but simplify and things will just feel simpler.

> **Learn:** There are tricks that will help you avoid frustrations and then tips on how to deal with them. The following paragraphs should help with both. From then on just know that frustrations diminish quickly with your own experience.

Tangles

When I talk of tangles I am specifically referring to the line getting caught up on things. Below are some tips on avoiding and dealing with the most common types of tangles.

Tangles during setting up: After you tied the line to the rod tip, when you start extending the rod, rather than let the line completely go and form a belly in front of the rod tip, keep the line in of your hands as you extend the rod. Make sure the line is running between your fingers or hand rather than tight, which would cause the rod tip to bend and potentially break. This will keep the line in control at all times.

Tangles while moving: There are many methods to manage your line while moving and each has their pros and cons. When moving a longer distance or through tight brush, collapse the rod and wind the line on a spool or with one of the line management systems discussed earlier. If moving a short distance keep the rod extended but make the line form a spiral around the rod by making the tip spin.

Tangles while casting: The main causes I have observed for tangles on the rod while casting are when the line is allowed to fall behind the angler during their backcast or when the angler moves the entire arm forward (rather than down at the elbow) on the forward cast. If the stop on the backcast is too long the fly will fall lower than the tip of the rod and tangle on the rod. Make sure your pause is very brief and almost instantly move the rod tip to cast the line forward.

The other cause for this tangling is easy to address and very common. If you are running into this problem frequently, see if you are moving your entire arm forward when casting. You should be moving your arm at your elbow up and down and avoiding moving the entire arm forward on the forward cast.

If the line tangles on the rod, there is a very simple trick that will get the line free 8 out of 10 times it happens: simply lift the rod tip up to point it to the sky.

Most often the line and fly will slide down to your hand and often free itself before you even touch it. If it doesn't come down to your hand or free itself automatically, keep it pointing up and collapse the rod to bring the tangle to you. Avoid, at all cost, the temptation of shaking the rod or pointing the rod tip down as that will worsen the tangle.

If the line catches the rod, do not shake it or point rod down.

Simply point the rod up and the line will come down to your hand.

Snags

Snags, which I define as the fly getting caught on things, will happen less and less as you gain experience. Avoidance of snags is absolutely key; there is no real secret to it but to be aware of your surroundings and then modifying your cast slightly to fit the obstacles above, behind or in front of you.

In case you do get the fly snagged there are different ways to get your fly back depending on where the snag is or what type of object is the cause of the snag.

Snags behind or above: These are the most common. We don't have eyes behind our heads and so it is easy to get caught on trees behind or above us. The main cause is not being very aware of where the tree is. Develop a habit of looking up and over your shoulders whenever you arrive at a new spot, move your body position (e.g. facing upstream to facing across stream) or move even a few inches up or down stream.

Once you know where the branches of trees are you can modify your cast to fit the situation based on what I shared on the casting chapter.

Snags in front: When there are potential snags in front of you, it may be a good idea to start with the fly landing closer to you and then progressively getting the fly closer to the intended spot. The more familiar you are with your rig the more you can go straight to your target while avoiding the potential snag.

When we misjudge the distance to our potential snag, the fly and line will end up going over a small branch. The best way to get your fly back is to treat every cast in front of you as a successful cast: stop the rod in front of you and don't pull it back. If the fly is over a branch, then very slowly and calmly pull it back and the fly will usually slide over the snag rather than catch it. If you pull it fast, the hook will do what it is designed to do and catch the object.

Snags at the end of a pool: Don't forget to look for potential snags at the end of a pool or run when you are fishing. We must recast before the fly hits a snag, such as a branch. If the fly gets snagged, remember to pull it back in the direction it was coming from (usually upstream) rather than up or downstream.

"The Fishing Tax"

One summer I found myself fishing with Dr. Ishigaki in a very tight stream in Japan. The stream he chose that day was tighter than any we had explored until then. It was small and covered with a lot of trees hanging over the water; I braced myself. The foliage and overhanging branches provided plenty of shade from the hot sun and kept the water cooler. The downside was that we were losing a lot of flies to the trees.

Every so often I'd see Dr. Ishigaki looking up and behind him to see what was keeping his fly from returning to the water. Sometimes he would get them back quickly. But I admit I took some comfort in knowing that even the most experienced angler I knew was not free from the snags around us.

As he tried to retrieve one of his snagged flies he noticed me looking at him. He tried a few ways to get the fly back to no avail. Finally, knowing there was no way to get the fly back, he collapsed his rod, put the rod tip inside, and pulled the line firmly to break the tippet off. He then turned to me, pointed at the lost fly and said "fishing tax!" while laughing heartily with his usual good sense of humor.

In fly-fishing nothing is certain but the occasional snag.

Getting the Fly Unstuck

Your fly will eventually get snagged. It happens to the best of us. When it does, there are two things you can do: Free the fly or break it off.

If your fly gets snagged on a branch or rock take a second to observe how it is caught, which direction it was coming from and what kind of object snagged your fly.

First, see if you can notice the direction the fly was coming from and pull the fly away from the direction it was traveling. Try a couple very quick and snappy flicks with your rod pulling away from the snag. It's important that the first tries be very quick but not strong attempts to pull the fly loose. A slow and firm/strong pull, or a long pull just makes the situation worse as the hook will set deeper into the wood.

Try a couple very quick and snappy flicks with your rod pulling away from the snag.

It's important that the first tries be very quick but not strong attempts to pull the fly loose.

It is usually easier to get the fly back from thinner branches of deciduous trees like oaks and willows, so I try a bit harder with those trees. I usually give up more quickly and move to the next step when my fly catches an evergreen such as a pine or spruce tree. If the fly gets snagged on a rock, try several very rapid shakes; getting the line to shake rapidly and repeatedly for a few seconds can often free the fly from rock snags.

If all else fails you may need to break off the tippet. To do so, collapse the rod until you can get the tip of the rod inside the handle segment. You may need to walk in the direction of the snag, and occasionally raise your arm to be able to collapse the rod. Place a finger on the rod opening to keep all the pieces inside, and pull on the line to break off the tippet.

It will be rare, but if you can not collapse the rod to put the tip inside and pull on the line with your hand, then you may need to use the rod to break the tippet. This is pretty rare. To do so, point the rod at the snag and pull it in a straight line to break off the tippet. It's important to do this only if absolutely necessary as segments can get stuck together.

Don't Leave Flies Behind

Several years ago I was fishing on the Firehole River in Montana's Yellowstone National Park after our annual Tenkara Summit. It was getting late in the day and I had moved away from the group to fish on my own for a bit. As I turned a bend in the river I noticed something hovering 20 feet above the water. It was flapping its wings and moving erratically up and down. I realized it must have been a bird so I moved quickly to get closer to it. It was a Clark's Nutcracker.

The poor bird was stuck in fishing line!

He was a bit too high for me to reach him, but I had an idea for how to free him. Using a technique I had created to retrieve my fly on a few occasions, I put the tip of my rod over the branch where he was stuck, with the line on the other side of the branch. I brought the rod down leaving only my main line over the branch. By pulling the strong line I was able to bring the branch down a few feet.

The nutcracker had a small nymph stuck in his beak, tippet was wrapped around his feet with a small fly also caught on his foot. The nutcracker had seen the "insect" dangling in the air and tried to eat it. Unfortunately he got caught in fishing line and barbed flies. The bird continued to struggle for a few seconds but I was soon able to catch him and hold him. I untangled the tippet and removed the flies, cursing whoever left those flies there and feeling awful for occasionally leaving flies and tippet behind too.

Once free the nutcracker flew to a branch 10 feet away and puffed up as if trying to get warmer. I stayed there watching him for several minutes, a bit shaken, reflecting on our collective impact on birds and other animals when we break off tippet and flies.

The sun was down and darkness was not far away. Had I not come around that bend just when I did, the nutcracker would have likely died an agonizing death. Ever since that experience I have tried a bit harder to get flies from snags, my own flies and others that I see left behind too.

Jeffrey Rueppel

Presentation Techniques

One of the key concepts of tenkara is that technique is more important than gear. As you have read previously many tenkara anglers use fewer, or even one, fly patterns and then learn how to present the fly in different ways.

In fly-fishing, the most common way to present a fly is to let the fly drift with the current as if it were a dead bug. This is called the dead-drift. But fly presentation is another area where tenkara shows us there is a different way of thinking about fly-fishing.

While the dead-drift is also the most common technique we use with tenkara, there are different techniques we can use to entice fish to bite. In Japanese they use the term "*sasoi*", which translates as "invitation". We can use our rods to impart motion, make the fly stop or move in ways that will invite a strike.

The 5 Main Techniques

After years of observing different techniques used by tenkara anglers in Japan, I was able to distill them into the five main techniques below.

> **Dead-drift:** let the fly drift with the currents as if it were a dead bug. Follow the fly with the rod tip.

> **Pulsing:** impart movement on the fly by moving the rod tip up and down. The reverse-hackle fly pulsates, opening and closing

> **Pause:** pause the fly in select spots for a couple of seconds by having the rod tip upstream or directly above the fly.

> **Pause-and-drift:** pause the fly upstream from a fish and let it drift a foot or two toward it, pause and drift, pause and drift...

> **Pulling:** pull the fly one to two feet at a time across a stream or river toward your shore, or upstream.

These are foundational techniques. As you'll learn in this chapter, there are variations to each technique. And anglers can combine techniques together, or perhaps even create their own.

Dead-drift

The idea with the dead-drift is to drift the fly in currents as naturally as possible along where food would normally drift to fish. The dead drift probably comprises at least 80 percent of my fishing and should always be considered a good default technique.

If you are fishing facing upstream, cast the fly upstream and as it drifts down start lifting the rod to keep up with it. If you are fishing across a stream, cast across and keep the rod tip high; then follow the fly with the tip of the rod as it goes downstream. Lastly, you can also fish downstream with a dead-drift by casting closer to you and as the fly drifts down start lowering the tip of the rod.

Upstream dead-drift

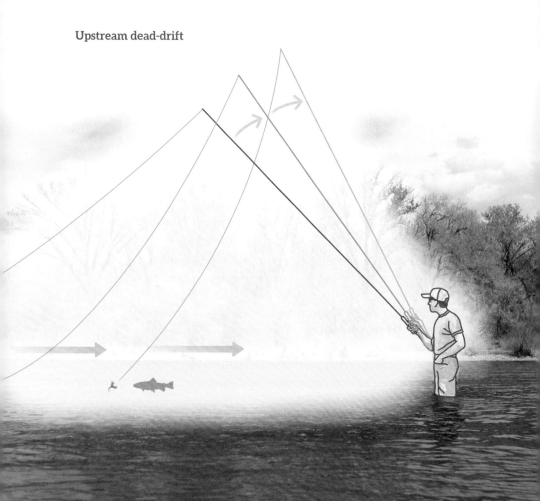

To perform the dead drift you'll want to avoid having much line laying on the water as currents will pick it up and "drag" it downstream at a different speed than the fly. This will make the drift unnatural and the fish suspicious.

WHERE TO CAST	Upstream, across, or downstream	
WHEN/WHERE TO TRY	Always!	
VARIATIONS	Slow the drift (Read: "Slowing the Drift" coming up)	
TIP	To improve your drift, push your arm out and downstream to make the fly go in a straighter line with the current.	

Across stream dead-drift

CURRENT

EXTEND YOUR ARM

Improving the Drift

The beautiful thing about not having to focus so much on line management and fly selection is that it frees us to pay attention to how we can improve our technique. One thing that will pay off is learning how to get the fly to drift more naturally and staying in a fish's feeding lane.

In streams, fish will often hold in a seam where food comes down with the currents in a fairly predictable way. As a fish sees the fly coming down it will make a simple calculation of where it will need to strike to successfully intercept the food.

IMPROVE THE DRIFT

10kara.co/25

When you keep your arm in one position and use only the rod tip to follow the fly, the fly will start swinging toward your shore. My technique was causing the fly to swing just enough to get out of the fish's intended strike point. The fish would rise but the fly was not where it should have gone.

To fix this, have your arm next to your body as you start the drift and follow the fly with your entire arm and rod moving away from your body and downstream. This will make the fly move in a straighter line with the current, as dead bugs will do, and will give the fish a better chance to intercept it. This technique is one of the most important "advanced" techniques I share with students.

Story: Slowing the Drift

Dr. Ishigaki and I were teaching a group of people during one of my visits to Japan. After a morning going over casting on the lawn and fly-tying in the lodge, we finally hit the water.

Temperatures had dropped overnight. The fishing was slow and we were catching fewer fish than we had a couple of days prior.

As usual, I cycled through a few techniques to see if something would work best. Nothing seemed to be working particularly well. So, I concentrated on finding the best-looking pockets of water to see if I could entice a fish out of them.

I found a whirlpool behind a large boulder. While the stream was very clear I did not see a fish, but I figured there had to be a fish there. I cast my fly, which hung in the pocket of water, circling around in the whirlpool for 2 or 3 seconds. Then a fish came up. The small amago came to my fly so slowly it seemed to just float toward the surface rather than swim to take the fly. At least I finally had a fish.

Knowing the fish were moving slowly I thought about something I had done in the past, I worked on slowing the drift of my fly. I followed the fly with my rod tip, similar to a dead drift but with the rod moving more slowly than the speed of the current. I essentially kept the tip of my rod just slightly upstream from the fly as I followed it. This seemed to work well.

Between Dr. Ishigaki and our seven students, they had caught two fish. I was already on my fifth. Two students came to me as I was landing a fish to see what fly I was using. It was the same as theirs, the simple Ishigaki kebari. "*Yukuri*," (slow) I said while fishing for words in my limited Japanese.

They looked a bit confused. I cast upstream and tried to show them the slower drift. It was subtle and hard to notice at first. On my second cast a light breeze blew my line lightly upstream slowing the fly for me even more. I continued following the fly slowly, and said "*yukuri kebari*" (slow fly). A fish came up. As sluggishly as the five before it it took the fly.

Slowing the drift proved to be particularly effective that day. All students caught at least one fish with that technique and I have continued to use it whenever the trout have been lethargic.

CURRENT

Pulsing

Many people ask why the *sakasa kebari* (reverse-hackle fly) has the hackle facing away from the bend of the hook. While there are other reasons I discussed in the fly chapter, my favorite reason for using reverse-hackle flies is that I can impart a pulsing motion on them.

The pulsing technique consists of pulling the fly up, which makes the hackle open up, and then relaxing the fly back down which allows the hackle to close. To pulsate your fly you will give the rod handle a very small amount of movement, which will translate into a larger amount of movement on the rod tip. One way to do this is to simply squeeze the rod handle with your ring and pinky fingers.

The number of pulses you will do will depend on the length of the drift. You may be able to do between 3 and 6 up-and-down pulses. Mr. Katsutoshi Amano sticks with one variation: a very rhythmic four pulses before re-casting.

WHERE TO CAST	Quarter upstream or across
WHEN/WHERE TO TRY	When dead drifts don't seem to be working. If water is running high/fast, or after sinking the fly
VARIATIONS	Small pulses or large pulses (not pulling the fly out of the water)
TIP	This should be a very controlled up-and-down movement, not erratic

Improving the Pulse

The pulsing technique can consist of very small pulses, say moving the fly only 3 to 6 inches at a time, or big pulses from 8 to 15 inches in up-down movement. In smaller streams and with smaller flies I will give preference to smaller movement. When the water is running high or murky I may do bigger pulses to make the fly more visible to fish.

To pulse the fly effectively, particularly when doing bigger pulses, try to have some of the main line or at least a few feet of the tippet in the water to anchor it all in place. Larger or more hackled flies will need less line in the water to work properly and prevent the fly from jumping out of the water.

It is important to keep in mind that the pulsing technique should be done in a controlled, rhythmic way and not in erratically. It's an up-and-down movement where the rod moves up and down in roughly equal amounts.

Very often when I show people this technique, they will make an erratic shaking motion. While that's not necessarily wrong, an erratic movement will make it difficult for the fish to grab the fly and even more difficult for you to set the hook.

A nice rhythmic up-and-down motion will have the benefits of allowing the fish to grab the fly more easily, and every up motion is also a potential hook set.

Story: The Sink and Twitch
Creating a New Technique

In 2010 Dr. Ishigaki came to fish with me in California. I had fished with him in Japan a few months earlier and was eager to show him some of my favorite waters. I was also very curious to see how easily the techniques he used to fish Japanese streams would translate to North American waters.

We spent a few days fishing different places around the Sierras. We went after golden trout in rocky canyons, large fish in big rivers, and then the scenic waters around Yosemite National Park.

As the host, I usually let him take the first casts. Plus, it was a relatively short visit for him and I could fish these waters anytime.

At one point we came across a very slow-moving pool of water. The sun shone down on it to reveal a small hover of rainbow trout. We approached them very carefully, as stealthily as we could to not spook them.

Dr. Ishigaki cast the fly with minimal amount of rod movement also not to spook the fish. I anticipated a strike as soon as the fly landed "from heaven," but the strike didn't happen. He let the fly drift. No fish. He tried a few more casts and manipulated the fly in a few different ways, skating the fly on the surface of the water or pausing and letting it drift. Nothing.

He was ready to give up and move to the next area. While I was a bit hesitant to second-guess my teacher, I asked if I could give it a try. I could see the fish were moving a bit, and possibly feeding, indicating they were not spooked by something and should be willing to take a fly. Plus, I had an idea, a combination of the drift and pulsing techniques that I had successfully used before.

I cast my sakasa kebari and let it sink. The water was shallow and the current very slow. In about 10 seconds the fly reached the bottom. I noticed a couple of the trout circling the fly the way sharks will circle their prey. I then twitched the fly, making it pulse just enough to say, "I'm alive." The trout circled it again, a bit more frenzied this time. With one more twitch the fly became irresistible. I saw one of the trout opening its mouth and my fly disappearing. I set the hook, brought a trout to hand and we all got to see its brilliant colors.

Hold for **1-2 seconds**

CURRENT

Pause

This technique involves pausing the fly in one place for a couple of seconds. To pause the fly, you can keep the rod tip upstream from the fly to stop it in place or keep the rod tip high and the line off the water if casting in very calm pockets. This can be a very effective way to coax stubborn fish.

Pick spots where you think fish may be hanging, such as in front of rocks, by weed-beds or in calm pockets of waters and whirlpools behind rocks. If you see different spots near each other, it may not be necessary to re-cast the fly, but just to angle the rod and make the fly skate or drift to a second position and then pause it there for a second..

WHERE TO CAST	Across, quarter downstream, or directly downstream
WHEN/WHERE TO TRY	In front of boulders and other structure (including submerged boulders), whirlpools and in slow pockets of water.
VARIATIONS	Rod tip high will make the fly pause on or near the surface of the water; rod tip low with line in the water will pause the fly below the surface.
TIP	Use light upstream winds to blow your line and stop your fly in place.

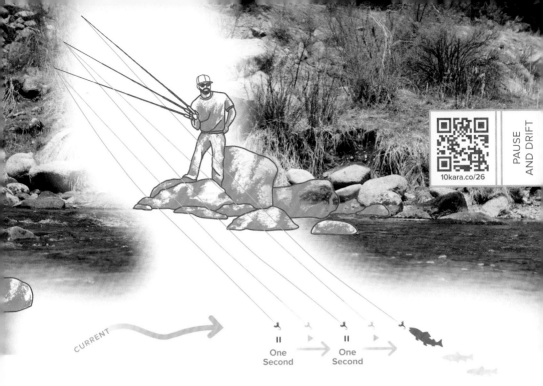

CURRENT

One Second — One Second

Pause-and-drift

The pause and drift can be seen as a combination of the first two techniques and is probably one of my favorites, but I use it often enough to mention it separately. The technique consists of briefly stopping the fly in place, with the rod upstream from the fly, and then letting the fly drift 1 to 2 feet, stop it again, drift, stop, drift... The pause is usually shorter than in the pause technique.

The pause-and-drift technique is best executed in a rhythm. One good way to execute this technique is to make a circle with the rod tip. Move the rod tip up in a circular motion and briefly stop on the upper and upstream part of the circle to make the fly pause. Then complete the circle to let the fly drift and briefly stop at the downstream and bottom part of the circle. Repeat a few times as you follow the fly with your arm also moving downstream.

WHERE TO CAST	Across, quarter downstream, or directly downstream	
WHEN/WHERE TO TRY		In front of fish-holding obstacles such as rocks, weed beds, or large submerged rocks. Spring creeks.
VARIATIONS		Raise the rod tip to closer to the surface, or lower the rod tip to fish below the surface. Vary the distance and tempo between pauses.
TIP	Push arm out and downstream to make the drift go in a straighter line with the current.	

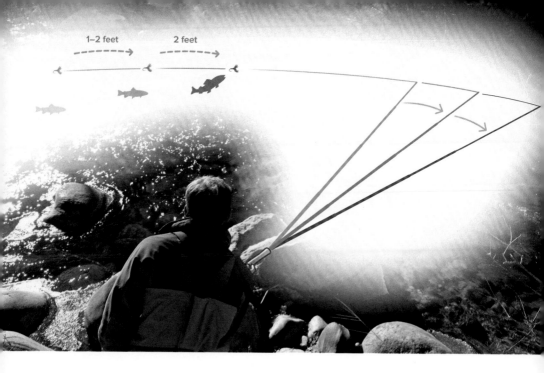

1–2 feet   2 feet

Pulling

The pulling technique gives the fly a lot of action by pulling it between one and two feet at a time toward the shore or upstream with very brief stops in between pulls.

The main difference between the pulsing and the pulling techniques is that while pulsing is done in an up-and-down manner, pulling is done sideways or upstream. The pulling technique can also be seen as the opposite action of the pause-and-drift; here it is actually a pull-and-pause. If you already fly-fish, this is a bit similar to stripping streamers.

To perform the pulling technique, have your rod close to parallel to the water. Also, keep line in the water; the line will serve as an anchor so that the fly doesn't come skipping out of the water. Just like with pulsing, practice this with a rhythm rather than erratically.

WHERE TO CAST		Quarter upstream, across or downstream.
WHEN/WHERE TO TRY		In high, fast, or murky water. When fish are aggressive and very active.
VARIATIONS		Faster or slower, shorter or larger pulls depending on how aggressive the fish may be.
TIP		Pulling produces best results when used with larger flies. Avoid pulling downstream.

When to Try Different Techniques

I normally begin a day of fishing by cycling through different techniques and seeing if one of them stands out as being most effective that day. If one technique didn't stand out over the others I will typically dead drift my fly three or four times in a pool or seam, often from downstream or from the side. If the pool looks promising but no fish has taken my fly, I will try the same pool from a different angle with a different presentation. If nothing happened on that pool, I'll move on and try a different spot.

The dead-drift is the technique I use the most, perhaps 80 percent of the time. Learning how to get the best possible drifts is paramount in tenkara. If I have one advice for improving your fishing, it is to observe how the fly drifts in different currents and working to get it to drift as naturally in the feeding lanes as possible. A terrific resource to learn more about currents is Jason Randall's book, *Moving Water: A Fly Fisher's Guide to Currents*.

When I see submerged boulders I like to pause the fly in front (upstream) of them, or pause it farther upstream and let it get closer by doing the pause-and-drift. I also like pausing the fly in very calm pockets or whirlpools, essentially letting the fly hang in a spot for a while. I like the pause-and-drift technique when fishing spring creeks with weed beds; it seems like fish will see the fly slowly coming toward them and will be invited to come out of the weeds to take the fly on the pause.

Pulling the fly across currents works well in larger pools of water when using large flies and when fish are very active. Pulsating the fly is always a fun technique to try as it can trigger the predatory instincts of trout and other fish.

But remember, just like with flies, it is important not to second-guess your technique too often. Letting the fly stay in the water longer and presenting it as if it were a dead bug are always two good bets.

Variations
The techniques presented in this chapter are the foundations of tenkara techniques. We can apply variations in speed and amount of movement to every technique. And techniques can be combined as well.

Rod Tip High/Rod Tip Low
Besides varying speed and distance of pulls and pulses, the two main variations for all the techniques presented here are to keep the rod tip high and line off the water or to lower the rod tip and placing some of the line in the water. When the line is off the water entirely and the rod tip is high, your fly will be on or very near the surface. When the line is in the water and the rod tip is very low, the fly will ride below the surface of the water. Knowing this will allow you to present the fly in different water columns.

10kara.co/27

Rod High

Rod Low

Rod tip high and line off the water: fly close to the surface

Rod tip low and some line in the water: fly below the surface

Creating a Hatch

The idea is to create the effect of a hatch or high bug activity where bugs are repeatedly dipping in the water and sometimes dropping and drifting. Cast the fly multiple times in one area without letting it stay in the water.

After casting the fly between 5 to 10 times, let the fly drift in that spot.

Swinging the Fly

This technique is usually featured in books on western fly-fishing. The idea is to cast across or a quarter downstream and let the fly swing toward your shore with the line stretched out. While I have caught fish this way a few times, because this technique requires the line to be stretched out downstream from the angler at the moment a fish takes the fly, the rod will not bend and sometimes the tippet can break. It is also a bit harder to hook fish this way. But, it is worth knowing you can do it, and some anglers really like swinging their fly.

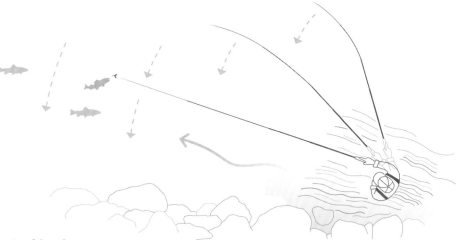

Looking Away

The most underrated yet effective technique we have at our disposal is to look away from where your fly is. It is a particularly good technique to try when you are losing hope and think you will not see a fish that day. Being distracted, talking to a buddy, or looking at a bird is a surefire way of getting fish to bite your fly. But, you must genuinely be looking away; fish seem to know when we pretend to look away. Be forewarned though, that hooking fish with this technique can be difficult.

Sinking Unweighted Flies

Most tenkara anglers use unweighted flies. My favorite thing about using flies with no added weight is their versatility. And, as always, versatility helps keep tenkara simple. With unweighted flies, we can use the same fly to reach different water columns by relying on technique rather than changing our rig.

Further, there is no need to buy, carry, use or lose split shot.

Whatever you put at the end of your line is completely up to you. It's okay to use weighted flies, or even put weight on your tippet. But, I have found that not using weight has really forced me to learn how to use currents to take my fly where I wanted it to go.

The limitation of not using weight is that we can not sink our fly deep and fast. However, with the techniques below we can sink the fly to the majority of fish we will encounter. Yes, the occasional fish may be out of reach with this limitation, but who has ever claimed to be able to reach every fish in the water anyway?

Plunging

The primary and most efficient way to sink a fly is to use plunges or channels where the currents will take your fly down for you. To use this technique you will rely on plunges or fast channels in a stream to sink your fly for you.

First, identify the places where currents are going over boulders to form plunges in the water. Then cast upstream from the plunge or fast water channel. Keep most of the line off the water in the beginning, and as the fly starts traveling toward the plunge start lowering the rod tip and placing more line in the water. As soon as it hits the plunge, lower the rod tip and get more of your line in the plunge or fast water channel. As the fly starts getting pulled down keep up with it by lowering the rod tip progressively. Keep the line relatively tight through the process.

If you are doing this correctly, you will see the line staying in place at the plunge. It will seem to be stuck for a moment. A few seconds later you will notice the line spin around in a circle and then move downstream. At this point you will start raising the rod tip and following your line downstream. Keep the line tight so you can detect strikes in case a fish takes your fly.

Submerge Fly

Deeper

Not every current is the same. Some will make the effect of plunging very obvious, others will be subtler and yet others will push your line out and not work well. The timing and depth of the plunge will depend on the speed of the currents. When you see a boulder sticking out of the water, there will often be a small plunge or fast water channel on either side of the boulder; try the technique on both currents and notice the differences.

In the beginning it will be difficult to tell if you are in the plunge or if the line is stuck on a rock below the surface. When you first start trying this technique, when the line stops or seems to tighten, lift the rod and see if the line starts moving again. Chances are the line was caught in the hydraulics and not on a rock. But, a quick lift will reveal whether you are caught in the currents and your fly was in the process of sinking or whether you were caught on a snag or perhaps on a fish.

After the fly has sunk, follow the fly with your rod at the same speed as the current for a dead-drift, or perform an up-and-down pulsing movement as it drifts downstream.

10kara.co/28

PLUNGING

Natural Sinking

You can get the fly to sink by casting far upstream and letting it naturally sink. While that may not take the fly as deeply as you want the first time you have the option of repeating the drift without recasting to get even deeper on a second or third pass.

Cast as far upstream as you can for the feeding lane you want, and let the fly drift down. As the fly starts moving downstream past the rod tip, start lowering the rod tip to continue letting the fly sink naturally as far as it will go. When the fly gets near the end of its reach (but not at the maximum reach you have), put all the line in the water and point your rod tip down, practically touching the water.

Then, with the rod tip pointing down and the line in the water, slowly pull the line upstream to start a new drift. It important to not pull the line too fast or to raise the tip of the rod since either action will cause the fly to ride up to the surface too fast. Let the fly drift and sink naturally this second time. Repeat as needed.

You can also identify micro-features such as tiny whirlpools and subtle currents and get them to help take the fly deeper. Start paying attention to how your fly and line behave when they hit small variations in currents. With time you'll see how these features can assist in carrying the fly down for you.

Length of Drifts

When it comes to length of drift we need to take into account whether a pool or section would require a longer drift to get the fly in front of fish. But, we must also pay attention to the length of drift that will allow for the best possible presentation of the fly.

Whenever the currents allow, aim for longer drifts as long you can present the fly well and where fish are likely to be. The benefit of a longer drift is that we may get the fly to go by a larger number of fish.

However, in smaller and shallower water it may be better to have shorter but better drifts and to break the stream into smaller sections to accomplish that. Shorter drifts, between 3 and 6 feet long, have the benefit of concentrating the time our flies spend in front of where fish are most likely to be rather than just in the water.

Dr. Ishigaki's research

Hisao Ishigaki is not a physician, nor does he have a PhD in fishing, although he might as well. Instead, he gets his "Dr." title by having a doctorate degree in the field of vision studies. When he started learning tenkara, Dr. Ishigaki applied his knowledge of scientific methods to conduct fishing experiments. Here's how he describes one of his first experiments during his early days learning tenkara:

> "[When I started tenkara fishing] I couldn't catch many fish, but I still thought it was a very fun way of fishing. So I started thinking hard about why I couldn't catch fish. I just assumed that fish held bait longer in their mouth but spit out flies right away. Out of curiosity, I decided to conduct an experiment about how quickly the fish would spit the fly and how fast a fisherman could react.
>
> I went to a hatchery that had three ponds, one with amago (a Japanese trout), one with iwana (a Japanese char, similar to trout) and one with rainbow trout. Using photo sensors connected to a hookless fly, I analyzed how long a trout held the fly in its mouth before spitting it out. First, the fly was held right on the surface of the water. A fish would jump to it, hold it in its mouth, and spit it out. Then I did an experiment with anglers to measure their reaction time between seeing a flashing light and trying to set a hook with a fishing rod.
>
> The average time for the fish to spit out the fly [placed on the water surface] was 0.2 seconds, but the shortest reaction time for a fisherman was 0.3 seconds. In other words, by the time someone reacts to the visual cue of a fish, it's usually already too late because the fish has already spit the fly out. So, I thought the best way to catch a fish would be to make the fish hold the fly in its mouth longer. The only way I thought would increase the time a fish held the fly in its mouth would be to have the fly in the water, not on the surface. Doing an experiment with the fly placed under water, the time a fish held the fly in its mouth increased to 0.6 to 0.7 seconds."

We all hook fish with flies on the surface. That could be because some fish hold the flies in their mouth longer than others; sometimes fish hook themselves and other times we see a fish before it gets to the surface and react just in time to hook it.

Dr. Ishigaki thinks the reason trout spit the fly out faster when taking it from the surface is because they feel the line when it breaks the surface tension of the water. When the fly is submerged fish don't feel the line since it has already broken through the surface film. The conclusions are that subsurface presentations may increase our chances of hooking fish; but also that no matter how much experience we have, we will all miss the occasional strike.

Detecting Strikes

"Strike" conveys both the fish taking the fly and our reaction to it by setting the hook. It is the moment we live for in fly-fishing. This is when our hearts beat faster and a quick jolt of adrenaline shoots through our veins.

There are many cues anglers use to detect strikes: line stopping or subtly tightening, flashes and shadows in the water, a fish jumping to grab the fly, and feeling the pull on the rod. Strike detection can only improve through experience. While I can share what I typically look for when fishing, it is important to experience it. With time you'll become quicker at recognizing signs that a fish may have taken the fly and will become quicker at reacting to these signs.

Different waters and situations may require different techniques for detecting strikes. For example, in murky water it is difficult to see fish below the surface, so watching the line is usually the way to go. On the other hand, very clear water is more conducive to watching for signs of fish in the water, such as a flash or the white in a trout's mouth as it opens to take your fly.

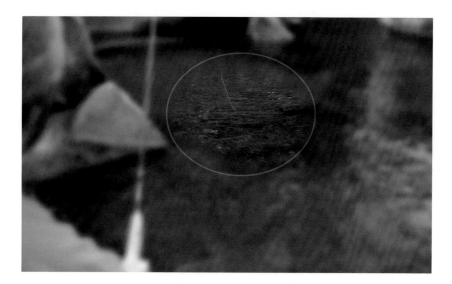

Watch Everything
It may seem funny to start talking about watching everything before watching for specific things, but that's how it works best so I will start here. I will give you specific things to watch for in a minute.

While fishing keep your eyes on the perimeter around the end of your line. I typically keep my eyes on the end of my line but focused a couple of feet past it. From the end of the line, I focus my vision a couple of feet in a straight line past the end of my main line.

Knowing that with a four-foot tippet my fly should be somewhere around its vicinity, I concentrate on a 4-foot perimeter around the end of my main line. I am watching for unusual things and reacting to everything that could be a sign of fish taking my fly: line tightening, line stopping, line moving upstream or outside the current, a silvery flash, a dark shadow, a white mouth opening, or my fly disappearing.

Get in the habit of reacting by lifting your rod tip slightly at anything that happens near your line.

See Through the Surface

In the course of introducing people to fishing I have noticed most people do not naturally try seeing through the water but rather look at the water. Seeing beyond the surface of the water is a very important skill as it will allow you to identify features and find fish. It will also help you detect strikes.

Seeing through the water is more than looking past glare. Rather, it's about getting our eyes to focus on what's happening below the surface. If we take out a camera with auto-focus and try getting a picture of a stream with relatively fast-moving water, the camera will focus on the bubbles, foam, and reflection on the surface while the rocks, sand and fish at the bottom will be out of focus.

It takes using a camera with manual focus to capture what's below the surface. Our eyes, like a camera, will naturally focus on the surface and we must make an effort to see what is happening beneath the bubbles and reflection. With time focusing on the deeper water columns becomes automatic.

Watch the line...

Line tightens...Set the hook!

Exercise: When you go fishing next time, take a moment to see what you can identify below the surface. Get your eye to focus on the bubbles and foamy lines on the surface of the water first. Then, focus on the rocky bottom. If it is a deeper pool with submerged rocks, can you focus on them instead?

Watch the Line

When the water is not very clear or if there is a lot of glare you need something to indicate a fish has taken your fly.

Fly-fishermen use a variety of accessories known as "strike indicators" (a.k.a. bobbers), to help them detect strikes. I mention these here to let you know they exist and to answer a common question: "Can I use strike indicators with tenkara?" The answer is yes you can, but I believe you don't need to. The tenkara line is a great strike indicator when you know what to watch for. It is very sensitive to strikes, I believe fish hold the fly a bit longer compared to strike indicators and using the line allows you to reduce the number of items in your kit.

It is important to keep the line tight as you fish with tenkara. Watch the line as it drifts. Focus on the small kinks and curves on the line. If the line stops drifting or the small kinks straighten, just lift the rod tip to tighten the line more and set the hook.

Many times people think their flies may be snagging submerged rocks, and they may be, but learn to react to anything that could be a fish.

Exercise: For a couple of fishing outings, focus exclusively on the line. Have your eye focus on it and it alone. Notice the subtle tightening that may happen as the line drifts and the fly touches a rock or gets caught in a whirlpool...or a fish strikes. When the line tightens, or stops its drift even slightly, make it tighten a bit more to develop the reflexes needed for setting the hook consistently.

Feel
It is important to strive to keep the tenkara line tight at all times. Often we may not be consciously focused on the water, perhaps our minds are wandering off even as we continue to fish and look at the water. It's okay; we all lose ourselves momentarily when fishing. The best way to wake up from these moments of trance is with the feel of a fish at the end of the line.

I find this is when most beginners successfully hook a fish. It's action and reaction without any need for conscious decision-making. Just like how you yank your hand away from a flame, when you feel a fish, your reflex will naturally set the hook.

Anticipation
Anticipation is present in every drift of our fly. Every time the fly passes by a very promising spot and you feel that a fish may take it, lift the rod slightly to tighten the line. There could be a fish.

When some of us anglers feel that we set the hook because we anticipated a fish, I believe it may be more due to us picking up on very subtle cues such as the line acting a bit differently or a small amount of vibration that came through the rod.

Luck

Occasionally we all start picking up the rod to re-cast, or move to a new location, and are surprised to feel a fish at the end of the line. Enjoy the fight.

Setting the Hook

When using tenkara all that is required to set the hook is a slight tightening of the line. At any sign indicating the possibility a fish took your fly, just lift the rod tip slightly to tighten the line. Once you tighten the line if there is a fish you will feel its vibration; if the line seems to have stopped tighten it a bit more and if it doesn't move it is a snag, otherwise you'll feel the vibration of a fish.

If there was no fish on the end of the line, you'll simply not feel a resistance, but since the motion required to set the hook is relatively light, your fly should not skip out of the water and you can continue the drift.

Note, the motion required to tighten the line and set the hook is to angle the rod tip back a bit rather than lifting the handle of the rod.

If you are new to fly-fishing you will find setting the hook with a tenkara rod to be very easy. If you are an experienced fly angler, it may take a little getting used to since you will not be pulling a line with your other hand, and the strike will take less effort than you are used to.

Exercise: To practice the motion required to set the hook, next time you are fishing and your fly is in the water, try pulling the line tight with a size-12 reverse-hackle fly. If the fly comes out of the water and jumps by more than a couple of inches, you're probably pulling too hard.

Landing and Handling Fish

"So, how do I reel in a fish if I have no reel?"

That is by far the most common question we hear when introducing people to tenkara. But I always like to respond that in many years of selling tenkara I have never once gotten a phone call from a customer saying, "Hey, I just hooked a fish, what do I do now?"

Landing a fish with tenkara may be one of the most intuitive parts about this method of fishing. When a fish is pulling on your fly and trying to get away, you'll know exactly what to do by pulling it back toward you. It's all about action and reaction. The goal is simple, to get the fish to your hand or net. And, without a lot of moving parts, bringing the fish in will be as natural as pulling it toward you.

During my tenkara demonstrations when I am asked how to land a fish with tenkara I always try to find a child in the audience to demonstrate. Without any explanation, I give the rod to a 6- or 7–year-old, then I grab the end of the line and tug it as if I were a fish. The child's imagination transforms me into a real fish and I ask, "If I'm a fish, how do you bring me to you?" Without over-thinking the child reacts to my pull by pulling back, and slowly they bring me within their reach. At that point, if the line is setup longer then the rod, they would grab the line and try to get me closer.

It's important not to overthink it. Years ago someone asked me that question during a demonstration. I couldn't find a child and ended up handing the rod to an experienced fly angler. I pulled on the line and asked the gentleman, "So, how do you bring me in?" He paused for a couple of seconds, looked up and down the rod, and then proceeded to lower the rod handle to the ground and started collapsing the rod segments to get to the line. Before anyone in the audience could think that's how it is supposed to be done I stopped him and let him know he was too smart for his own good. He was overthinking the whole thing.

Fighting Large Fish

Once a fish is hooked, then the fight is on. With a smaller fish, things will be very straightforward; just angle the rod back and bring the fish toward you. But things can get exciting fast with a larger fish, so I'll share a few tips for fighting them. These tips should help bring the fish quickly to the net.
The first run of a fish is the most crucial moment of the fight. That's when the fish has the most strength and is most eager to test your limits and try to get that sharp object off its mouth. Once the first run is under control, the rest becomes relatively easy, and you'll enter into a back-and-forth tug-of-war. Tenkara rods are designed to fight fish. The bend of the rod may scare you when you hook your first larger fish, but don't panic, that's normal.

It is very important to keep the rod pointed up at least at a 45-degree angle; this will allow the rod to continue to bend to absorb the strong pull of a fish. If you point your rod at the fish, or allow the fish to pull the rod down too much, you lose any shock-absorbing function a rod may serve and the fish will break off. Keeping the rod angled up has the additional benefits of pulling the hook up and keeping the fish on as well as forcing the fish's head to come up into the air, an unnatural position that will weaken it and help the angler land it quickly.

It is also important to use your arm and sometimes your legs to help in the battle. When a fish is pulling keep your rod pointed up but move your arm with it a bit to help absorb its strength.

Doug Heggart and Daniel play doubles with large browns in Wyoming.

Dr. Ishigaki has talked about fighting larger fish by using the term term "*Inasu to Kawasu*", a term from martial arts that refers to the idea of giving in slightly when the opponent is strongest and reacting more strongly when the opponent is weaker. When a fish wants to pull go with it, then pull when you feel you can.

In time you'll develop the sensitivity for fighting fish, especially the larger ones. Don't be timid with bringing the fish in toward you but do it gently and calmly. It's a bit like trying to get a stubborn dog to move with you. You must guide it to where you want it, gently and calmly but also firmly.

Tip: In my experience, most tippet breakages are caused by a bad knot or bad tippet. As a friend of mine once said, "Tie every knot as if you were about to catch the biggest fish of your life." This means tie your knot carefully, lubricate it with some saliva to make sure the line doesn't lose strength due to friction when tightening the knot, and give it a nice test pull to make sure it's all looking good and strong. I recommend using 5X tippet when fishing in most places, or 4X if targeting larger fish.

Tenkara guide Steve Conrad about to land a good size brown trout in Colorado.

Landing Technique

There are a few tips that will help with acquiring good technique for landing fish. Good technique will make it so that you can land large fish about the same as smaller fish, and it will allow you to land fish while using short lines just as well as using longer lines.

When you first start tenkara fishing, use a line that is about the same length as the rod plus 4 feet of tippet. This gives you a chance to learn how to land a fish in an intuitive way. To land the fish, you will angle the rod tip back, then reach for the line and bring the fish as close to you as you can, in calm water, then net or grab the fish. This is the technique I use whether my line is about the same length as the rod or twice as long.

The only difference is that with a short line I'll grab the line and have the fish on hand or in my net immediately. With a longer line you'll have to hand-line the fish to bring it closer to you. This takes a bit of getting used to, which is why I recommend starting with shorter lines and progressively using longer lines if you see a need for them.

Keep your arm close to your body, avoiding extending your arm up and/or behind you. This will give you greater control of the fish and allow you to more easily reach the line when needed.

Hold the rod at the handle. Some people may want to make the rod shorter, either by holding it above the handle or by collapsing a segment. Counter-intuitively, shortening the rod will make landing the fish more difficult as a shorter rod will make your line comparatively longer and harder to manage.

Bring the fish to calm water. Even a small fish may feel harder to land when you are fighting it in heavy current. So, the first step is trying to guide a fish to calmer water, where it will be easier to fight it and easier to land it at the end.

With good technique a larger fish can be landed in the same way as a smaller fish, though with more adrenaline in your veins I'm sure. And, contrary to what some may believe, it is not necessary to fight fish for a long time or throw the rod in the water to bring a larger fish in. In fact, because there is no line to take away, it is often quicker to land large fish with tenkara than with a rod and reel.

Whenever possible bring the fish away from heavy currents and into calmer water. You may want to move downstream with a fish while pulling it in a perpendicular orientation to the currents toward the calmer water at the shore.

Fighting the fish toward a perpendicular orientation to the current will redirect some of the energy the fish is exerting into moving it to the calmer water. Keep an eye out for obstructions behind you that could catch your rod or line.

There are two techniques for reaching the line. The first is to keep the rod in front of you and then point it back until the line is within reach in front of you.

The second is to point the rod back while also angling the rod slightly toward your empty hand. At this point you can do a sweeping motion with your empty hand to find the line and start hand-lining the fish. Once again and with both techniques, it will be important to keep your arm close to your body.

10kara.co/29

LANDING
A FISH

Technique 1: Reach for line in front of you

Technique 2: Point rod towards free hand and grab line

If you are having a hard time landing fish with a tenkara rod, I have noticed two main things that are often the problem. The first problem is usually raising the arm high up, so keep the arm closer to the body. The second main source of frustration with landing fish is when the angler points the rod away from their empty hand, or by angling the rod too far out of the reach of their empty hand.

It is important to have the rod pointing up but angled slightly toward the middle of your body, in the direction of your free hand. In other words, if you are holding the rod with your right hand, you need to point the rod toward your left hand to be able to grab it. Keep in mind that with a very long rod, it takes a very small angle variation at the handle for the rod tip to point way outside of your reach.

Lastly, it is very important to keep the line tight at all times. This part is generally pretty easy with line of a length similar to the rod since the rod will flex and unflex depending on how the fish is behaving. With long lines you will need to work on keeping the line tight even when you have grabbed the line. Read the section on hand-lining for some tips on that.

Hand-lining

When the line is longer than the rod you will need to use your hands to bring the fish in. Reach for the line with your empty hand, hold it, and then use your rod hand to help pull line in.

When I first started using long lines, I lost a lot of fish during this step, especially the smaller fish that wiggled rapidly and freed themselves from my barbless hooks. Here are some tips to help you land more fish :

Pull the line up, rather than straight toward you. One reason using a pole for fishing is so effective, and a reason I have heard "angling" is called angling, is because the rod keeps the line up at an angle. The upward pressure caused by the rod ensures that the fish stays hooked rather than pulling the hook out of its mouth. You can successfully land fish by pulling them straight toward you, but I have found pulling the line upward seems to help me lose fewer fish.

Slow and steady. Jerky movements and hasty pulling don't help bring fish in. Bring the fish in slowly and steadily and in calm water when possible.

Be prepared to let it a large fish run again. As you start bringing in a larger fish slowly and steadily, you'll need to be sensitive to how strong the fish may be and may need to let it take another run. Do not grab the line too firmly; grab it with your hands relaxed and let the fish take a very short run while keeping the line in your hand, or occasionally let the line go completely and repeat the process. This does not mean playing the fish to exhaustion, and often is only needed to be done once, but be prepared to let the line in your hand go if you feel the fish may break off.

Bring it close. Bring the fish as close to you as you can. It is tempting to try to reach the fish as soon as it is within reasonable reach but this will cause you to try to hand or net the fish in a stretched out position.

That kind of stretching means loss of control: if the fish jumps or makes an unexpected run to either side of you, you will be in a bind and may lose it. Even with pretty large fish, it's best to bring it as close to you as you can before netting it or grabbing it.

Don't throw the rod in the water!

If you've heard that should you hook into a large fish with a tenkara rod the best option is to toss the rod in the water because rods may break otherwise, I would recommend ignoring that advice, which is based on old lore and old technology and should not live on. Throwing your tenkara rod in the water is neither recommended nor necessary.

Back in the day, say some 300 years ago, tenkara and western fly-fishing looked nearly identical, with neither anglers in Japan nor those in Europe using reels. Fishing rods at the time were made of wood or bamboo. Those rods used to break more easily than most modern rods and were much harder to repair or replace. When anglers of that period connected with a very large fish, they had to make a choice: fight it out and almost certainly break the rod and also lose the fish; or save themselves the trouble by tossing the rod and hoping for the best. I'm sure this didn't happen very often, but it was a reality due to the tackle used at the time.

Fast forward a few hundred years and materials have come a long way. Nowadays rods are made of carbon fiber, a much stronger material. We design tenkara rods so that they can bend deeply and absorb the high pressure applied by large fish. Tenkara rods are still not designed to target large fish, but if you happen to hook into one, keep steady pressure, move downstream, follow my advice on techniques for landing fish, and land it without tossing your rod in the water. A well-designed tenkara rod can handle it. Of course, if you choose to throw your rod in the water, we will be here to sell you another one.

Big Fish on Tenkara

Tenkara is not designed to catch very large fish. It is a method that was designed to catch mountain trout. It also happens to work fine for panfish and bass. Plus, so far it has proven to work fine even with fish most Japanese tenkara anglers would never expect to be caught with tenkara rods, such as carp, salmon, monstrous pike, or steelhead. All those have been caught on our rods. If you are curious, do a quick online search for whatever fish you are interested in and tenkara to see what comes up.

No fishing equipment is designed to target every fish size, and tenkara does not attempt to do that. But it is wrong to think of it as just a "very small fish" technique. The following are two good examples of large fish that were successfully landed with tenkara. The fish below were quickly landed and then released in great shape back into the water.

Tenkara guide Shaun Lezotte with a 29-inch pike in South Dakota.

Kendra Veil

Ryan Jordan

Handling Fish

Congratulations! A fish has taken your fly, you fought it well, and now it is within reach. Whether we will catch and release the fish or keep it, I believe it is important to treat our "prey" with dignity.

Bring the fish in quickly rather than exhausting it, and then minimize handling of the fish. Fish have a layer of slime that coats their skin and protects them from problematic threats such as fungus, parasites, and more. It is important to always wet our hands and minimize touching fish to avoid removing that protective layer. And never place a fish on dry ground.

Next, keep the fish in the water as much as possible. I have really become a fan of using a fishing net for this reason. I can place a fish inside the net and keep the fish in the net and in the water to remove the hook.

Never squeeze a fish or touch its gills. The area of a fish's body that protects its vital organs is pretty soft and squeezing that part of a fish can directly harm its internal organs.

If someone is taking a picture of you with your fish, get the photographer to compose the image before you lift the fish out of the water. Hold the fish (gently and from below) closely above the water so that if it wiggles itself free it will fall back in the water rather than dry ground.

Remove the fly by holding the hook with your fingers or forceps if the fly is farther inside its mouth. Barbless hooks make this step much easier.

To release the fish, place it back in the water with its head facing the current so water can flow back through its gills to help it can regain its energy. Hold the fish gently in the water until you feel it is ready to go on its own power. Avoid releasing it in very strong currents, but do release it where water is flowing.

Tenkara began with commercial fishermen of the Japanese mountains catching fish as a food source. They used tenkara as a means to an end, a way to earn a living. In their day fishing was so good that catching 100 fish a day was common, and they kept them all. Luckily, we no longer need to keep every fish we catch.

After several trips to Japan and being taken aback by how few fish there are in some of the streams there, I have become a much stronger believer in the importance of catch and release and responsible taking.

People should not be denied the right to eat the occasional fish that they catch. I will eat the occasional fish too but reserve that treat for places with an abundance of fish and a scarcity of anglers, such as when I'm backpacking. If you'd like to read or listen to my thoughts about responsible keeping and catch-and-release practices, scan the QR code on this page.

When I asked Mr. Yoshimaru Shotaro if it was easier to learn to fish when he started, he responded with a tone of nostalgia, "There were a lot more fish back then."

Celebrated angler Lee Wulff once said, "The finest gift you can give to any fisherman is to put a good fish back, and who knows if the fish that you caught isn't someone else's gift to you?"

That we can enjoy fishing as a sport rather than a way to sustain ourselves is a great privilege. Fishing is but an excuse to get outdoors and enjoy nature in a very intimate way. Through tenkara we get to find out what lurks beneath the surface of streams, rivers, and lakes. We get to satisfy our hunter and gatherer instinct but with the choice to keep it simple and to enjoy the catch without the need to take.

10kara.co/30

C&R (& K) PODCAST

Glossary

Amago: name of a Japanese trout, *Oncorhynchus masou ishikawae*, with red spots on its body. The name is thought to come from *"ame"* which means rain, and *"ko"* which means child, thus "rain child". Also, name of one of Tenkara USA's rod, a 13ft. 6in. "big fish" rod.

Dapping: a technique in which the fly is lowered into the water, or taken by the wind.

Drag: drag can be used in reference to current drags, where, when line is laid on the water currents will drag the line downstream. It can also be used in reference to the drag on a reel, which is used to slow down the unspooling of line.

False-cast: casting back and forth in the air before dropping the fly in the water, used to help dry the fly if you desire to make it float more or to help gauge the distance while casting. Not used much with tenkara.

Forceps/Hemostats: small pliers that can be used to pinch things like hook barbs or to grab things when our fingers are too large such as hooks that get too deep inside a fish's mouth.

Iwana: name of a Japanese char, *Salvelinus leucomaenis*. Also, name of one of the best-selling tenkara rods in the market produced by Tenkara USA.

Kebari: Japanese term for an artificial fly, literally "haired hook."

Level line: level diameter line used as one of the main line options in tenkara.

Lillian: from the term "lilly yarn", lillian is the braided material permanently connected to the tip of the tenkara rod and onto which the line is tied.

Mend/Mending: to fix the drag created by currents pulling on the line. Doesn't have to be done with tenkara.

Nippers: nippers are small cutters used to cut line or tippet.

Sakasa: Japanese term that means "reversed", used to describe the sakasa kebari, or reverse-hackle fly.

Conversions

The measurements in this book, such as rod and line lengths and fish sizes will be given in the imperial system. Tippet diameter uses the "X" classification.

Some of the most popular lengths of rods are rounded in the imperial system to keep numbers cleaner – for example, the standard length for a tenkara rod in most of the world is 360cm, which would be 11.81feet; I took the liberty to call them 12 foot rods. Luckily we are not dealing with a very exact science here! Here are some conversions that may come in handy for this book. Measurements with an * are not accurate conversions, but rather I took the liberty to use more commonly available dimensions when those exist:

Lengths

IMPERIAL (US)	METRIC
12 inches (= 1 foot)	30 cm
4 feet	1.20 m
10 feet *	300 cm
11 feet *	330 cm
12 feet *	360 cm
13 feet *	390 cm
14 feet 7 inches	445 cm
1 mile	1.61Km

' = feet or ft   " = inches or in   (e.g. 14'7" would be 14 feet and 7 inches)

Weights

IMPERIAL (US)	METRIC
1 lb	0.45 Kg
5 lbs	2.26 Kg
6 lbs	2.72 Kg

Tippet - approximate as measurements may vary by brand and type

X	Diameter (mm)	Diameter (inches)	Breaking Strength (kg)	Breaking Strength (lbs)
6X	0.127	0.005	1.5	3.4
5X	0.152	0.006	2.3	5
4X	0.178	0.007	2.9	6.4
3X	0.203	0.008	3.7	8.2

Other Resources

Videos

Our videos are available on tenkarausa.com/videos
and via our YouTube channel youtube.com/tenkarausa.

10kara.co/31

VIDEOS

10kara.co/32

TENKARA CAST

Podcast

The Tenkara Cast™ is available on our website and also
on itunes: tenkarausa.com/podcast

Other books on tenkara

Simple Flies and *Tenkara Today*
Both books by Morgan Lyle

Tenkara fly-fishing – Insights & Strategies
by David E. Dirks

Tenkara, Radically simple, Ultralight Fly Fishing,
by Kevin C. Kelleher, MD with Misako Ishimura

Simple Fly Fishing
by Yvon Chouinard, Craig Mathews and Mauro Mazzo

Tenkara Angler
A magazine curated by Michael Agneta

Trout from Small Streams - 2nd edition
by Dave Hughes

Tenkara Magazine
An annual publication, sharing the tenkara story™, and featuring words and
images by the tenkara community, visit tenkarausa.com/magazine

For a current list of books available on tenkara and other recommended
reading, please visit tenkarausa.com/literature

Other online resources

The Tenkara USA blog features posts on technique, philosophy, fishing in Japan and more: tenkarausa.com/blog

Tenkara-fisher.com, created by Adam Trahan has excellent information on traditional tenkara

Tenkaragrasshopper.com, a blog by Graham Moran

Tenkaratalk.com, a blog by Jason Klass has a great variety of posts

Tetontenkara.blogspot.com, a blog by Tom Davis

For further online resources, which are always changing, visit tenkarausa.com/online-resources

Events

The Tenkara Summit is an annual event hosted by Tenkara USA to bring the community together to share knowledge on the tenkara method of fishing.

10kara.co/33

EVENTS

The Tenkara Summit normally features guests from Japan and several presentations, fly-tying and casting demonstrations and more.

For a list of other events around the globe visit tenkarausa.com/events

Shop

Since 2009 Tenkara USA has been creating and refining its tenkara rods, tenkara lines and more. You can get all you need to start fly-fishing simply at tenkarausa.com or at a dealer near you.

10kara.co/34

SHOP

1% of the sales of this book and all Tenkara USA gear are donated to environmental organizations that help care for trout habitat.

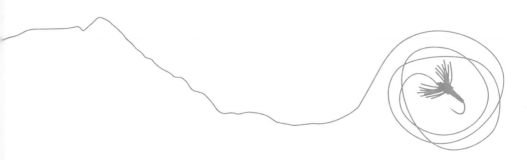

Acknowledgments

My wife, Margaret Kuwata, stood by me through the stress and uncertainty of creating a new business based on a concept no one had ever heard of, in the middle of a great recession and just as we started our lives together. I'm so grateful for her support through it all and her company on many good fishing trips. Of course, I would also have never discovered tenkara if Margaret and I hadn't met.

I am most grateful to those who instilled in me a great passion for fishing and the outdoors from an early age. My parents, Miguel and Lorelei Galhardo, showed me the importance of the outdoors and the fun that could be had by spending time outside. I cannot even begin to imagine a life without the outdoors.

My grandfather, Wilhelm Baumeier, taught me how to soak in the air of nature, and the importance of learning. He inspired me to want to lead a simple life. He would have been a tenkara angler if he could.

Our staff members, in particular Thomas "TJ" Ferreira and John Geer, always "held the fort" when I needed to concentrate on the book or to go in search of inspiration away from my desk. They have passionately helped introduce tenkara to the world.

Jeremy Shellhorn, the illustrator and designer behind this book, must be thanked not only for the design work you see here but also for his determination in helping me get this book done. His vision, incredible eye for detail and design skills show through every page of this book.

I'm also extremely grateful for the tenkara anglers in Japan who have welcomed me as I went "in search of tenkara" and have so unselfishly shared their knowledge with me. A special thank you to Mr. Katsutoshi Amano, Mr. Yoshikazu Fujioka, Mr. Masami Sakakibara, Mr. Yuzo Sebata, and Mr. Eiji Yamakawa for helping me understand the 10 colors of tenkara. And, most of all a special thank you to Dr. Hisao Ishigaki for sharing so much knowledge and time and inspiring me to share tenkara and to keep it simple.

The community that sprang up around tenkara has been one of the coolest things to witness. I am incredibly humbled and grateful to all the people who have taken an interest in tenkara over the years. Your interest allowed tenkara to become a word in today's fly-fishing vernacular.

There is a long list of individuals in the tenkara community that have supported my work over the years. It would take many pages to list all of our "ambassadors" and supporters in this book. To those of you who have helped us at sport shows, volunteered at the Tenkara Summit, contributed to our blog and the Tenkara Magazine, participated in our podcast and videos, mentored me and have gone fishing with me, a most heartfelt THANK YOU!

Lastly, it should be shared that this book project has lingered heavily on my shoulders for years. I knew it had to be done the moment I decided to bring tenkara outside of Japan. Yet, between creating the business and initiating other projects I kept putting this book off. Between false starts and multiple drafts, this project has been in the works for about four years. But the time has come to just get the book out.

In 2016, with the majority of the manuscript done, I put the project on Kickstarter. This was a good way to get the pressure I probably needed to get it published. Thank you to all who supported the project before it was finished and let me know you wanted this to be out there. It's a bit late, but it is here.

Tight lines,

Daniel W. Galhardo
March 2017

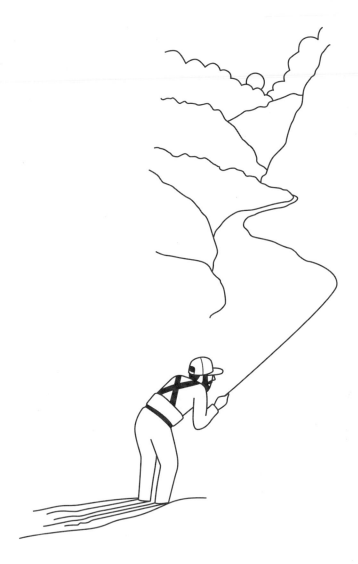

Tenkara fishing is very simple, which makes me feel I am a part of the mountains.

YUZO SEBATA